R65937

KV-445-886

745.5 MUR

UCA
university for the creative arts

9780975730348

Rochester, Fort Pitt, Rochester, Kent, ME1 1DZ
Return on or before the last date stamped below. Fines will be charged on overdue books.

WITHDRAWN FROM STOCK

Craft Unbound

MAKE THE COMMON PRECIOUS • KEVIN MURRAY

New Art Series Editor: Ashley Crawford

CRAFTSMAN HOUSE

First published in Australia in 2005 by Craftsman House
An imprint of Thames & Hudson Australia Pty Ltd
Portside Business Park, Fishermans Bend, Victoria 3207
www.thamesandhudson.com

All rights reserved. No part of this publication may be reproduced or transmitted in any
form or by any means, electronic or mechanical, including photocopy, recording or any other
information storage or retrieval system, without prior permission in writing from the publisher.

Any copy of this book issued by the publisher is sold subject to the condition that it shall not by way
of trade or otherwise be lent, resold, hired out or otherwise circulated without the publishers' prior
consent in any form or binding or cover other than that in which it is published and without a similar
condition including these words being imposed on a subsequent purchaser.

National Library of Australia Cataloguing-in-Publication data.

Murray, Kevin, 1966–
Craft unbound: make the common precious
ISBN 0 9757303 4 7
1. Handicraft in art. 2. Art, Modern. 3. Arts and crafts movement
4. Artisans. I. Title. (Series: New art series)
745.5

Editing: Astrid Judge
Design: Terence Hogan
Production: Imago
Printed in Singapore

Author's Acknowledgments:
Thanks greatly to the artists in this book for choosing to share with us their experiences, ideas and
images. Thanks to their families and those teachers who played a critical role in nurturing their
talents. And thanks for the commitment of Thisbe Purich and Nalda Searles, the editing of
Astrid Judge, the faith of John Ross and the care of Moss, Shirley and dear Naomi Cass.

Frontispiece:
Louiseann Zahra: *my most tender and respectful love*, 2002, silver, 6 x 6 x 5 cm, photo: Justin Bernhaut

Australian Government | **Australia Council** for the Arts

This project has been assisted by the Australian Government through
the Australia Council, its arts funding and advisory body.

CONTENTS

'Hands make the world every day.'
Pablo Neruda

Roseanne Bartley: *Southern Bloom,* 2004, tennis ball (Merri Creek parklands), sterling silver, stainless steel pin, 5.5 x 6 cm, photo: Terence Bogue

MAKE THE COMMON PRECIOUS

By Kevin Murray

Introduction

There was once a familiar order to things. On one side was the supermarket and on the other was the art gallery. There was the world of common things to be used up and discarded, and the realm of precious objects to be appreciated into the future. The meaningless cycle of consumption was counterbalanced by the collection of treasured objects. But this cultural economy has become stagnant as art becomes increasingly insular and detached from everyday life. Consumption continues to accelerate while art risks being locked into the fashion cycle.

A generation of radical Australian makers is challenging this arrangement by bringing the profane world of consumption into the sacred halls of art. Theirs is not merely a conceptual exercise. There is no Duchamp-like cleverness about their use of found objects. These craftspersons express a renewal in the elemental energy of creation, reaching back to the mysteries of material transformation in alchemy. They are breaking through.

This is a distinctly Australian phenomenon, and we need to gather these makers together to appreciate their work, learn about its origins, and understand its meaning. What is the relationship between beauty and rarity that their work confronts? Let's begin to examine this question with the broad brush.

The lay of the land

To make the common precious is to work against the grain. The identification of value and rarity is self-evident. It governs the way we see the world and how we transact with it. According to Gestalt psychology, we perceive the world by dividing it into figure and ground: the lone object stands out before the common background. By taking the common for granted, we can focus our attention on the singular.

In the English language rarity is almost always expressed using words that carry a

Facing page:
Stephen Gallagher
Shagged Jewel Pendant 2003
acrylic sealant (extruded), stainless steel mesh (heat treated and pressed), 925 silver (oxidised), pure gold, cotton thread, akoya and cultured pearls, red coral, bakelite
14.5 x 8.5 x 1.3 cm (pendant only)
Photo: Terence Bogue

positive connotation – words such as 'extraordinary', 'special', 'rare', 'incomparable' and 'noble'. Whereas what is common is valued negatively, as in 'ordinary', 'average', 'mundane', 'usual', 'pedestrian' or 'plebeian'. Accordingly, we will pay more for something that is exclusive, one-off or editioned than we would for goods that are mass-marketed.

This asymmetry is especially prevalent in the world of art. It seems obvious that the beautiful is necessarily exceptional. After all, art history is peopled by rare geniuses who produce rare masterpieces. Craft plays its own part in this story. In the decorative arts treasures such as the Fabergé Eggs are valued for their rarity as much as their craftsmanship. The value of an object is conditioned more by its supply than its simple use value.

But there are ways in which this natural order of things can be questioned. In a radical move the French sociologist Pierre Bourdieu argued that rarity is not the accident of beauty, but rather its cause.[1] We enjoy a masterpiece *because* it is rare. According to Bourdieu, art enforces a hierarchical society, in which value must be seen as limited to the few.

This view has its shortcomings. While providing a powerful critique of aestheticism, such arguments do not suggest ways of creating beauty that are alternative to the existing economy. To find these, we need to go beyond academic theory and explore the popular values that shadow elitism. The different manifestations of elitism provide us with alternative ways of understanding what Australian craftspersons are achieving today.

Throughout the history of Christianity, the gospels have often been used to support the Church's responsibility to the broad mass of people – 'The meek shall inherit the earth.' In contrast to the hierarchy of the Vatican orders such as the Franciscans make humility a life-long vocation. And, most radically, during the Reformation anti-elitist movements celebrated daily labour and the common tongue. A similar tension is present in Islam, in the opposition between the priestly Shiite and popularist Sunni versions of the religion. Beyond religion, popularism was given its most powerful expression in the revolutionary movements that culminated in Marxism. Given the declining significance of theology and ideology in the third millennium, where might an aesthetics of commonness reside today?

Facing page:
Fleur Schell
Temporal Sounds
(sound instrument with metronome) 1999
fine china, mixed media
70 x 20 cm

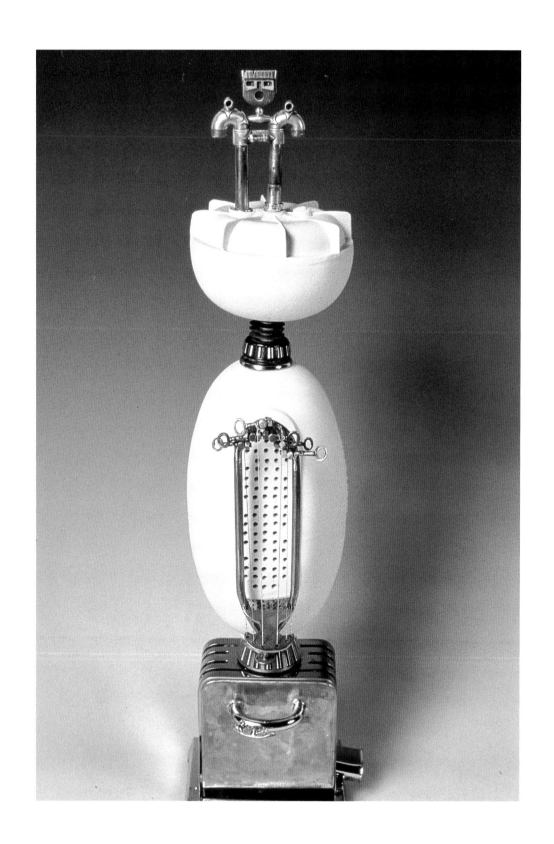

Sally Marsland
Flat Colour Brooch 2002
side-view, silver brooch fitting
epoxy resin, powdered pigment
5 x 6 x 1 cm
Photo: Terence Bogue

In Western society, there is alongside the mainstream economy of beauty a black market of artistic production.[2] The value of rarity is *reversed* when it is seen to be tightly controlled by a particular group. Thus there are negative terms associated with those who police rarity, such as 'elites', 'priesthoods', 'snobs' and 'cabals'.

The craft movement

Throughout modernity, craft has provided an alternative set of values to the positivist dream of technological advancement. At its most basic, craft is the transformation of common materials into precious works. Potters dig up mud which they shape and bake in the fire to make vessels for eating and drinking. The history of modern craft is characterised by a search for these elemental roots.

It was during industrialisation in the nineteenth century that craft emerged as a foil to modern capitalism. Reflecting a Protestant spirit, the English Arts and Craft movement of this period championed labour and decried bourgeois decadence.

Rarity was a significant issue for the movement's champion, John Ruskin. He admitted that certain kinds of rarity, such as a fine sunset, were legitimate as 'Nature's way of stimulating your attention'. However, if rarity became a matter of possession, then it was idolatry: there was no reason to value pearls above glass beads. So Ruskin wrote, 'If only the English nation could be made to understand that the beauty which is indeed to be a joy for ever, must be a joy for all.'[3] At the time, the craft spirit was identified as a northern phenomenon, with its origins reaching back to the historical struggle of egalitarian Anglo-Saxons against their Norman overlords.

In the twentieth century Western craft turned to the East. The English potter Edmund Leach introduced the values associated with Mingei, a Japanese movement of folk ceramics. These values emerged from a strain of Zen Buddhism that sought enlightenment in the here and now. A key text for Mingei practitioners was *The Unknown Craftsman* written by Soetsu Yanagi in 1931, which stated 'Why should beauty emerge from the world of the ordinary? The answer is, ultimately, because the world is natural.'[4] Yanagi's values were epitomised in the Kizaemon tea bowl. This sixteenth-century bowl was celebrated as one of Japan's most significant treasures. According to legend, the bowl was found in a Korean workshop, and produced by a regular worker in a moment of complete unselfconsciousness.

The roles were reversed in the late twentieth century. Crafts practitioners reacted against the earnestness associated with the Arts and Crafts movement, and with Japanese ceramics. Post-modern flamboyance and conceptualism, such as that inspired by the Italian designers Memphis, removed craft from its demotic base.

Meanwhile industrialisation entered the information era, which altered the basic economy of production. Today, the greater the number of people who possess a particular piece of software, the more valuable it is. As Pierre Lévy writes, 'Everything that flows from top to bottom in theological discourse should be viewed, within the technosocial system, as flowing from bottom to top.'[5] What was vertical has become horizontal – networks replace silos. While technological change has proceeded largely independent of the arts, it does alter the mindset in which the arts are perceived. Craft is just beginning to enjoy this new ground.

Poor cousins in the arts

Modesty of means is not exclusive to the contemporary crafts movement. The 'Poor Theatre' of Polish director Jerzy Grotowski evolved in the 1960s as a rejection of theatrical excess, such as lush sets and lavish costumes. It used austerity to bring the focus back on the unadorned actor. This process was extended into cinema with *Dogma 95*, the Danish movement led by Lars von Trier, which precluded sound tracks and editing in order to bring acting to the fore. For von Trier and other like-minded directors, to work with whatever is at hand promises to be a more transparent means for creative expression.

In the late 1960s Grotowski's Poor Theatre inspired an Italian art movement known as 'Arte Povera'. Influenced by American minimalism, a group of sculptors reacted against what they saw as a commodification of art, and created works that materialised a raw creative energy. Their process involved both found materials and spaces outside galleries.

For its main spokesperson, Germano Celant, Arte Povera was a distinctly European movement which contrasted with the futuristic and industrialised scene in America. As Celant writes, European progress 'is made up of elements astonishingly cobbled together, of deteriorated, ancient materials, excavated from the past and recycled according to intuitive, illogical visions.'[6] Arte Povera embodied the primitivism of Poor Theatre while articulating a specific message about the heterogeneity of European history. And it embraced the enigmatic.

Louiseann Zahra
Laid Out on Splendid Biers
(detail) 2003
second-hand white, yellow
and rose gold wedding rings,
glass, crystal, feathers, beads,
dried marigolds, brass,
bronze and silver
Photo: Justin Bernhaut

Tjanpi Toyota made by Blackstone women and conceived by **Kantjupayi Benson** desert grasses
500 x 200 x 120 cm
Photo: Thisbe Purich

The antipodean future

At first, there seems no place for a country such as Australia in Celant's scheme. On the one hand, our thin past does not reflect the rich palimpsest of European history. Australian history seems like a crust of colonialism built over a seemingly timeless continuity of Aboriginal occupation. And on the other hand, Australia is not gripped by the positivism of its American cousins. The cultural dynamic is more colonial in character. It is within the colonial story that we might find the ground for a distinctly Australian craft.

According to the colonial mindset, Europe is the rightful home of preciousness. In his book *The Australian Ugliness*, Robin Boyd holds up the north as a model: 'Yet in England, unlike America and Australia, there is always something of genuine beauty around the corner, a medieval church or a glimpse of field, hedge and honest stone-work.'[7] This Europe is studded with the precious jewels of its grand pasts.

Such 'colonial cringe' naturally evokes a republican response. There have been many strains of irreverent nationalism. In the 1990s the Sydney designers Mambo celebrated suburban values, typified in local wisdom such as 'The grass is always greener around the tap.'[8] Films such as *Muriel's Wedding* associate suburbanism with a free spirit and the sense of community; they foster a boisterous pride in being ordinary.

Australian folk craft reflects this popularism. Bush furniture celebrated the make-do practices of farmers who were isolated by the great distances of the outback. A kerosene tin became a chest of drawers. Likewise, the isolation of Aboriginal communities has encouraged an ingenuity of means. The 2001 television series *Bush Mechanics* celebrated the almost magical ability of the Walpiri people to keep cars going without the backup of tools and supplies. Australian popular applied arts have been forged by isolation.

Australia shares this celebration of the common with other ex-colonies, particularly in the south. Consider the most influential poet in South America, Pablo Neruda. He was ideologically committed to ordinariness. His *Elementary Odes* are rhapsodic verses in praise of ordinary things. In his Nobel Prize acceptance speech, Neruda claimed that 'The best poet is he who prepares our daily bread.'[9] The popularism of Liberation theology and leftist revolutions aims to continue the struggle first established against Spanish imperialism into the factories.

Parallel sentiments are being expressed across the Indian Ocean, where the African Renaissance upholds the value of collective tribalism against capitalist individualism. The post-apartheid generation of South African intellectuals is keen to turn the freedom struggle beyond the spectacle of mass riots to the matters of ordinary life. The author Njabulo Ndebele writes about the 'rediscovery of the ordinary' as the focus for political action: 'If it is a new society we seek to bring about in South Africa then that newness will be based on a direct concern with the way people actually live.'[10] Cultural energy in the new South Africa stems from township life, particularly music and craft.

There are clear differences between a majority White country such as Australia, and the racial profiles of nations in Africa and South America. Craft in Australia is located in galleries, where it is partly removed from its value in the market. Yet despite differences in culture and economy, all southern nations share the condition of seeming to live in the 'shadow' of the north, where the common things of our world are outshone by the precious imports from afar.

Eventually corrupted by modernity, the modest spirit of craft in the West seeks renewal from outside. In the past Western makers looked to the Viking north and pre-modern East. Now it is from the south that emerges a fresh energy.

'Poor craft'

The nineteen makers profiled in this book have chosen to work with materials which might otherwise be considered worthless. They have gathered remnants, packaging and rubbish that have no place in the economic system: they turn to whatever is at hand. This 'poor craft' is a particularly rich source of creative expression.

To speak of a 'poor craft' is to suggest a movement that is bound by common experience and ideas. But it would be premature to christen a new movement. As products of relatively modest backgrounds, the makers in this book share similar sensibilities, though their ideas about preciousness sometimes diverge.

These artists share a common story. They are like the last fruit of a native Australian tree that only grows in the wild. Their childhoods were spent in relatively free open spaces – if not gazing upon the open horizons of the bush then roaming the wilds of the outer suburbs. They grew up before television had absorbed recreational time, and so faced the rare challenge of learning how to create time themselves and to make virtue of necessity.

Relatively few of the makers moved in a straight line. While institutional training has been a critical part of their development as a craftsperson, most have gained ideas on their own. There are certainly common themes that emerge through the work of these artists; they share a spirit of invention and an interest in the alchemic transformation of materials, and many are engaged in a critique of consumerism. Together, they all seek forms of creative energy that are not bound by commodification. Better to have something roughly made from common materials than a slickly produced object that fits snugly into its niche market. While the artists gathered in this book share a use of common materials, their differences are also important. There are two opposed aims. One is the goal of overturning hierarchy, whereby common becomes precious – lead replaces gold. The other is the abolition of hierarchy itself, to make the precious common – gold is reduced to lead. The former tends to be more strategic in orientation, making a mountain out of a molehill. The latter is more modernist in approach. One overturns the pyramid; the other transforms it into a cube. There are reformists, and there are revolutionaries.

The differences between the artists in this book prompt much debate and questioning. I have grouped the artists according to their method of approaching the

Sally Marsland
*Why are you like this
and not like that?* 2004
vessels left to right: epoxy resin
(mixed with powdered pigment)
cast copy of a Guy Boyd ramekin;
found aluminium bottle with
plastic screw top, reanodised
black; glazed earthenware
5 to 25 cm high
Photo: Julian Hutchens

Nicole Lister
A Conventional Arrangement 2004
limoges porcelain, clayworks, MFQ
13 x 28 x 28 cm
Photo: Michel Brouet

ordinary. Each chapter deals with a particular group of makers. *Gatherers* draw from the Australian land to produce work, while *Fossickers* discover materials in manufactured environments. *Gleaners* use what gets left behind, such as packaging, and *Alchemists* look to the physical transformation of materials. *Dissectors* expose beauty through the act of destruction, but *Liberators* take the precious out of the gallery and onto the street. While representing a fresh, critical edge in Australian culture, each maker also demonstrates a growing inventiveness in the field of craft.

Like their cousins in Poor Theatre, these makers of 'poor craft' seek modesty of means as a way of renewing creative expression. As in the reality television program *Survivor*, makers are thrown back on their own craft to make works of beauty from what is at hand. And, as in the Arte Povera movement, found materials offer resistance to the dominant economic system, and allow for the spontaneous expression of identity. Ironically, both Poor Theatre and Arte Povera were inward focused and relatively unpopular art movements. 'Poor craft' seems different. In its reference to everyday life it seems possible that 'poor craft' will enjoy a broad audience, untutored in art theory. This is a rare moment for the art of the ordinary.

Chapter 1: GATHERERS

While the Australian landscape has been an enduring subject for artists, the stuff of the land itself has been relatively overlooked. Materials for creative expression tend to be found elsewhere, in pigments imported from Italy or fine Scandinavian timber. A new generation of artists is beginning to explore the poetry that lies in the land itself. From the common fruits of the land, these artists are creating works of very particular meaning.

Kantjupayi Benson

By labelling central Australia with the word 'desert', the science of geography does no favours to the region. Rather than the rolling sand dunes of deserts as conjured by a European imagination, Australia's semi-arid centre is ridged by mountains, dotted with trees and covered in grass. It is this verdant life of the centre which has spawned one of Australia's newest crafts – grass sculpture.

Located about a thousand kilometres west of Alice Springs, the cryptic Blackstone Ranges provide a backdrop to a string of Ngaanyatjarra communities, including Wingellina, Jamieson and Blackstone. As yet, these places have not attained legendary status in the world of Australian art – unlike Turkey Creek or Papunya. But the artists of these communities possess a unique creativity that gives expression to ancient stories using the materials at hand. Rather than representing their world through acrylic on canvas, these artists express their culture through the land itself.

The story begins with an organisation run by the desert communities themselves. Formed in 1980, the Ngaanyatjarra Pitjantjatjarra Yankunytjatjara (NPY) Women's Council coordinates cultural activities throughout the western desert. Through their *tjanpi* ('grass') program the NPY has developed various ways of producing and promoting grass crafts. By conducting basket-making workshops the organisation has fostered an accessible craft that draws on local knowledge, and provides a means of exchange both between communities and with the outside world. The NPY plays a coordinating role by distributing materials, buying up baskets (they attempt to purchase every one made), selling and marketing them. Many of the techniques have been developed by women in the communities themselves, such as unpicking old jumpers to incorporate woollen thread into baskets.

Kantjupayi Benson
collecting spinifex, Blackstone 2003

Kantjupayi Benson

Eagle Story 2003

wool, wire, human hair, raffia, gauze, found objects,
tjanpi (desert grass), minarri (woolybutt, E. Miniata),
wangunu (naked woollybutt, Eragrostis eriopoda) and
kutanu (greybeard grass, Amphipogon caricinus)
left: 67.6 x 50 x 59 cm
centre: 80 x 49.8 x 55 cm
right: 77.7 x 38.5 x 73 cm

Purchased with funds donated by Supporters and Patrons
of Indigenous Art, 2003
Courtesy of National Gallery of Victoria

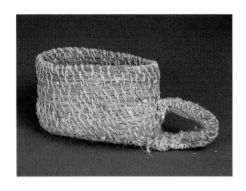

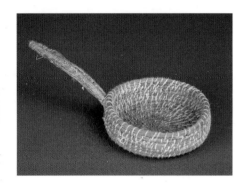

Locally NPY are also involved in the annual Alice Springs Beanie Festival, during which Aboriginal and White people gather to celebrate the common item of clothing that they use to protect themselves against the below-freezing winter nights in the desert. Crochet and basket-making are important sources of exchange in a society that otherwise retains an implicit apartheid division in the town.

As part of its promotional activity, the NPY is involved in overseas ventures. In the year 2000 a number of western desert women travelled to Hanover in Germany to weave a giant basket. In 2002 the women visited Manchester which was hosting the Commonwealth Games; they had been invited to give workshops in making animals from grass.

Most importantly, the NPY organises workshops through which new techniques and materials can be explored. Skills are constantly developing. Artists have been taken to the Koorong to learn South Australian indigenous weaving techniques. In 1995 a workshop was held in the western desert community of Tjukurla, and a number of White artists were invited to demonstrate alternative techniques. Among them was the West Australian fibre artist Nalda Searles, who along with the NPY art advisor Thisbe Purich had learnt to speak Ngaanyatjarra. Nalda subsequently spent time with many Aboriginal communities in the west and developed techniques of binding grass with thread that seemed to be both appropriate to the lifestyle and offered a new language of expression.

Nalda and Thisbe noticed that one artist in particular had taken grass beyond traditional basket-making into the realm of figurative sculpture. Kantjupayi Benson was a senior Blackstone (Papulankutja) woman who was interested in making art using a variety of means, such as paint from a tomato sauce bottle. Kantjupayi was the first artist to incorporate emu feathers into baskets, a technique that has since become very popular. By 1997 she had started making animals, such as lizards and dogs, from carved wood and grass. In 2001 she made work for a touring NPY exhibition called *Manguri*. Her piece was based on the woven rings women place on their heads to carry loads. It included a series of items of camp crockery, such frying pans, cups and billy – all out of grass. Kantjupayi seems to have a thing for grass.

Along with three other Ngaanyatjarra women, Thisbe and Nalda, Kantjupayi was commissioned to make some figures for an exhibition based on *Inma Kungkaran-*

gkalpa, the story of the seven sisters. *Kungkarangkalpa* was sung during the opening ceremony of the Sydney Olympics by women from central Australia. Unfortunately, the story was not explained in the commentary, but it continues to be told throughout Aboriginal Australia. Like the ancient Greek myth of Orion the *Kungkarangkalpa* story is based on the Pleiades star cluster and tells of seven sisters who are pursued by a love-sick old man. As the story is told in communities across the breadth of Australia, it imbues different features of the landscape with meaning. For the *Seven Sisters* installation Kantjupayi made the male figure Wati Nyiru, featuring hair string belt and headband, as well as a sister.

These grass sculptures are vigorously constructed. Kantjupayi uses a wide variety of material, including desert grasses, wire netting, handspun human hair, raffia and wool. The compositon is particularly dense; it is quite easy to be absorbed so much in the sheer materiality of the work as to forget it is a human figure. Standing back, the expressive features, such as fingers and nose, help spring the figure back into life. These are dynamic works.

Far from a lone figure, Kantjupayi is strongly embedded in her community. Born sometime in the 1930s, Kantjupayi has one son and two daughters. Two children are blind and she contributes all of her art income to them. Kantjupayi is part of an active community of artists including Ivy Hopkins, Jean Burke, and Elaine Lane, who are evolving their skills to meet the growing interest in their work.

Since her *Kungkarangkalpa* sculptures, Kantjupayi has made a suite of work interpreting stories and mythologies in grass figures. She has created pieces based on the 'Bush Banana' story and the 'Emu and Galah' story, among others. These works have been collected by the National Gallery of Victoria.

Kantjupayi's vision for grass knows no bounds. Like an alchemic quest, her idea of transforming the world into grass has reached epic proportions. For the 2005 Telstra Art Prize she conceived the notion of making an entire Toyota out of grass. There's much poetry in this monumental work. Making objects from grass gives Kantjupayi, her friends and family the excuse to venture out into the bush and gather materials. This is one of the pleasures of her practice. But to do this requires that most precious object in the bush, the Toyota Land Cruiser. Sales from Kantjupayi's grass works contribute to the funds necessary to purchase and maintain these vehicles. With her

Facing page and above:
Kantjupayi Benson
Details of *Camp Crockery*
installation in Manguri
exhibition, organised by
NPY and toured nationally
and overseas in 2001

Toyota made from grass Kantjupayi has taken a more direct approach.

Through the developmental work of the NPY council, an artist such as Kantjupayi has been able to realise a new language for expressing Australian cultural identity. Using the most common material of the desert – grass – she is able to give new form to the land's most precious legacy of stories.

Kate Campbell-Pope

Western Australia has produced a generation of fibre artists who have made the land their medium of choice. This has been achieved through dialogue between contemporary and indigenous crafts practitioners. Thanks to the influence of some key creative figures, the new fibre artists have found ways of using the rich flora provided by nature as a medium for expression. The story of Kate Campbell-Pope typifies the power of applying a natural medium using Western technology.

Kate Campbell-Pope grew up in the south-west Australian town of Albany, where she lived within five minutes walk of the beach. It was an idyllic Australian childhood of creative engagement with nature. She recalls exploring open spaces – endless sand hills; making mud-cakes in the drainage channels, and collecting shells on the beach. These were the ephemeral crafts idiomatic to beach life. She was taught by her sister's boyfriend how to make 'dribble castles' by carefully dripping wet sand between two hands. Clay could be collected close to the house and she was allowed to use it on the dining table. 'At six I remember thinking I would like to be an artist, although I didn't remember ever meeting one.' The beach provided a base of creative experience, though not necessarily a direct path into the world of an artist.

Like many artists featured here, Campbell-Pope first tried a 'serious' profession. She initially trained as an occupational therapist, and she continues to work in this field in various forms today. But in 1988 she enrolled in Art and Design at the Claremont School of Art, and eventually she found her way into Edith Cowan University. Since 1988 the Textiles department at Edith Cowan has organised annual bush camps. Students are initiated into the creative possibilities of the Australian landscape by being placed in a 'survivor'-like situation where they have to make work from whatever they can find.

These bush camps have been a critical meeting point for key figures in the West Australian fibre scene. They were pioneered by Nalda Searles, the seminal West

Kate Campbell-Pope
self-portrait at Baladjie WA

Facing page:
Kate Campbell-Pope
Working History 1996
installation
medical instruments, bandage,
grass, thread
100 x 60 cm
Photo: V. France

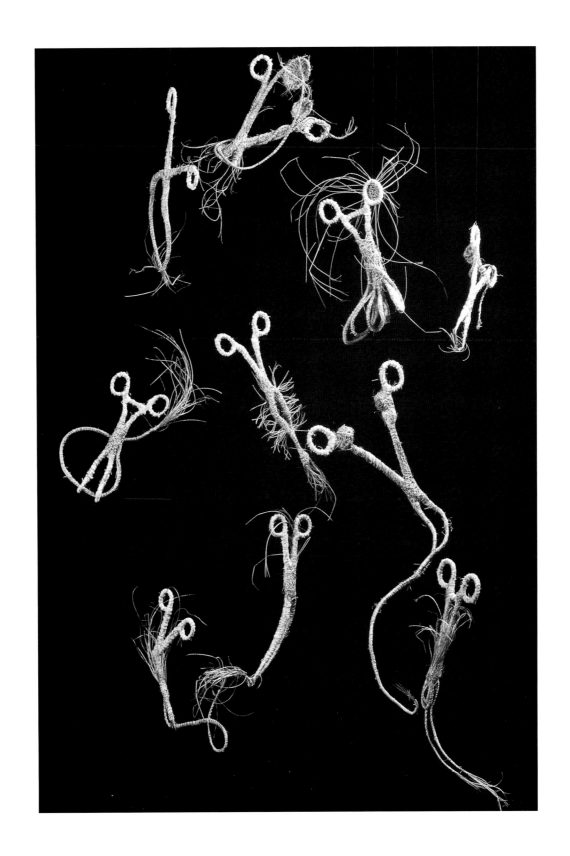

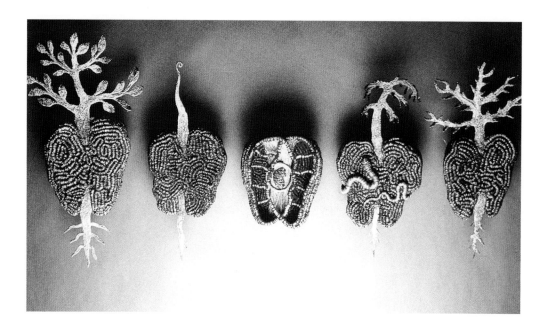

Kate Campbell-Pope
My Heart of Transformations 1998
stitched grass, fabric, wire
18 x 30 x 8 cm
Photo: Bill Shaylor

Australian artist who forged new techniques for applying needlecraft to local fibre. She had taken traditional basket-making techniques into more sculptural areas, embroidering found fabrics with flora. These techniques were proved useful in many Aboriginal communities in the south-west and desert. Searles was joined by Else van Kippel, who helped develop a new language of natural dyes. Other artists who were influenced by the bush camps included Cecile Williams, Bronwyn Goss, Maureen Landers, Ruth Hadlow, Rinske Car and John Parkes.

Western Australia provided a stimulating scene for an aspiring fibre artist. Kate Campbell-Pope formed a relationship with the Ngunga artist Joyce Winsley. Winsley had taken Nalda's techniques further along the path of reflecting natural materials. She was able to bind grass in sculptural form without the use of cotton thread. Her figures were entirely made of grass. Winsley unfortunately passed away in 2001, but Campbell-Pope retains close contact with her community in Narrogin.

For Campbell-Pope, grass appeals as a concrete medium of natural beauty. 'I don't like too many tools between me and what I am working with.' What particularly appeals to her is its everyday quality. 'I like the idea of making something out of what we walk over and walk over and don't notice.' Through grass, she brings the democracy of the beach into art-making.

Campbell-Pope's work reflects Joyce Winsley's very refined use of grass. Her grass surgical instruments express a delicacy that is belied by the raw materials from which they are made. The cold metal of medical technology seems the antithesis of the organic fibre that carpets the earth.

This medical theme continues in work based on human organs. The moist theatre of flesh is rendered in the dry material of grass. Looking at Campbell-Pope's work, it is possible to grasp the common material bond that links our living selves with the natural world we inhabit. The artist's fine working of coarse material is particularly exquisite.

Campbell-Pope is part of an active artistic community. She and other artists, such as Holly Story, are experimenting with what the land has provided in Western Australia. The bush alchemy of these makers, like that of Kantjupayi, has ambitions to render our specialised manmade world into the hair of the earth.

Ari Athans

Throughout the history of colonial Australia the quest for preciousness has been expressed most obviously in prospecting for gold. But this quest has in a sense represented a missed opportunity. Once discovered, gold is rarely enjoyed for its own sake. The quicker it is cashed in, the better. While opals are standard tourist fare, Australian jewellery rarely contains elements from its own land. One jeweller, informed by the gypsy heritage of her Greek background, has found a way of adorning bodies with elements of the land on which they stand.

Ari Athans in her workshop
Photo: Tim Kassulke

Ari Athans's story begins with the iconic tale of Greek migration, but arrives at an unlikely destination. Her parents migrated to Australia from the Peloponnesian towns of Patra and Kalamata in the late 1950s. They met and married in Sydney, three years later. Like many Greeks, Athans's parents began as factory workers and then graduated to serving take-away food.

Athans's mother left Greece with only a suitcase, which contained all her precious jewellery. She continued to collect precious things throughout her life, even her children's umbilical cords. Athans recalls the mystery of her mother's collection: 'Everything had its special box, and all three girls would gather around her and listen to the stories of each piece over and over again as we all claimed each object for ourselves. To this day I can still feel the power that jewellery brings to one's life.' Athans sees her

Facing page:
Ari Athans
Bloodlines 2002
hematite, red cotton
4 x 38 cm
Photo: Ari Athans

Ari Athans
Pebble Tools 1996
Nepean River pebbles,
stainless steel, nylon wire
12 x 7 cm
Photo: Ari Athans

Ari Athans
The Agate Family 2002
Queensland agate, sterling
silver
4.5 each cm
Photo: Ari Athans

heritage as including Greek Orthodox religious festivals, pagan rituals passed down from her gypsy grandmother (especially involving jewellery), the preparation and eating of food, and her father's socialist politics.

It was a long and winding path to jewellery. Athans soon became aware of her love of arts and crafts, but the sense of needing a serious career led her to take a degree in Geology, which seemed one of the most creative sciences. 'The idea of being outdoors looking at materials that were formed millions of years ago, and to understand how they got there, is truly astounding. So now when I work with gemstones or any geological material, you get a strong sense of permanence and timelessness about them.' Thus was laid the bedrock of her future career as a jeweller.

Athans graduated with a degree in Geology and worked in Queensland and West Australian mining towns. One job took her to Mount Isa in outback Queensland. Lead, copper, silver and zinc are mined there in one of the largest underground base metal mines in the world. Athans's task was to map and collate geological information using underground and drill core samples. The experience of fossicking took her away from her Greek heritage and helped her understand what it meant to be Australian.

Feeling stifled by the mining industry, Athans decided to take two years off to study Jewellery at Randwick TAFE (now Enmore Design Centre). 'I can still remember

Ari Athans
Tinga Creek Quartz-wear 2002
iron-stained quartz tumbled crystals,
brown silk, neckpiece
60 cm
Photo: Ari Athans

walking into that amazing TAFE workshop – and *bang* it hit me! I never looked back.' Athans remembers the critical advice offered by lecturer Robin Blau, 'to be true to the materials', which has guided her work ever since. She also studied Gemmology part time.

Athans's experience in geology and jewellery combined in an exhibition called *Stoneware*, which incorporated typical Australian lapidary into precious jewellery with alchemical associations.[11] Her *Bloodlines* necklace binds hematite with a red thread. The name of the mineral hematite is derived from the Greek word for 'blood', providing Athans with a link to her family heritage. Athans enjoys the way hematite can be easily polished and carved; she uses it widely for production jewellery.

More common than hematite is quartz. Athans incorporates quartz into rings that accentuate its crystallised quality. The rings hide the smooth, cut surface and expose the rough crystal. The wearer harbours a secret contract with the earth.

Today Athans works full time as a jeweller but continues her interest in fossicking. She retains a large collection of rocks, minerals and gemstones. She remains an active member of a lapidary club, from whom she sources stones.

Athans's creative practice embraces many techniques and issues. She often uses text to explore the collision between Greek and Australian identities. At a practical level, she runs a successful jewellery gallery and workshop in Brisbane.

Athans continues the journey that her parents began in leaving the Peloponnese after the war. Just as her parents treasured the precious remains of the life they left behind, Athans finds ways of valuing the world they found in the antipodes. She says, 'I see myself as someone who scavenges for raw materials that end up in the studio until they are transformed into a jewel to be worn.' From the rough new land, Athans makes work fit for her mother's jewellery box.

Damien Wright

Furniture made by Damien Wright is a critical testament to how we might understand Australia today. With sensitivity, passion and skill, Wright finds a place in our lives for previously overlooked native timbers. Trees such as gidgee, ironbark and desert acacias have been avoided for generations by craftspeople because of their difficulties – the wood is too hard, difficult to dry; it has an irregular grain and twisted shape. Yet Wright has been able to work with the contrariness of these woods and turn

Damien Wright

Above:
Damien Wright
Twins 2004
brigalow
280 x 80 x 40 cm
Photo: Terence Bogue
Private collection

Right:
Damien Wright
Surface Tension 2004
coastal sheoak
140 x 70 x 35 cm
Photo: Terence Bogue
Collaboration with Olivia
Griffith

Far right:
Damien Wright
Square In the Face 2004
and detail
ancient redgum, Gidgee
140 x 105 x 380 cm
Photo: Terence Bogue

'rubbish' into objects of authority. How has he done it? The journey begins, and ends, in childhood.

Wright's parents were Queenslanders of Irish and English Catholic stock. His father's family had worked in sugar mills and his mother's had run pubs. Damien's parents both became teachers and settled in Redcliffe, just north of Brisbane. Wright attributes his spirit of independence and self-sufficiency to his parents' rural character – 'very physical, inventive, self-reliant people'. They were Catholic socialists with 'a constant desire to question and shake'. When Damien was three they moved to Melbourne to escape Queensland's conservative political landscape.

The family found ways of maintaining their bush independence while living on the fringes of the city. They settled in an old orchard in the outer suburb of Ringwood. Damien's father encouraged him to make for himself whatever he needed. 'As an eleven-year-old I wanted a stereo, so my father bought me the electronic bits – including the turntable – of a stereo, and gave me an instruction manual.' Backyard activities were supplemented by family trips to central Australia. Damien's parents wanted him to learn about the desert and follow the research maps of explorers. For Wright, the quest to learn through experience 'just got under my skin'.

It took Wright some time to find his path. There was no initial promise at school – he even failed woodwork in Year 9. But he improved in Year 12 and enrolled in Arts at Melbourne University. Wright's passionate engagement did not fit easily with the academic environment – 'Felt like I was trespassing while I was there.' He challenged values of the time by taking football as a serious topic of cultural history. The subject for his Honours thesis was the relocation of the South Melbourne Football Club, and he later co-authored a book about the Footscray Football Club.[12] Such a line of enquiry earned Wright few points at the time, though sport history has since become a major field of research and teaching.

After university, Wright threw himself into the field of action, and played semi-professional football with the Victorian Football Association. But his enjoyment of physical challenge was often at odds with the spirit of the game. He describes being more interested in 'the grace of the moment' than the main source of popular interest, violence. His football career came to an end eventually when he broke his hand sending a punch in retaliation for a vicious kick. 'We had a baby and I couldn't work for three months. There was no joy in football.'

Meanwhile Wright had started making furniture out of driftwood. The odd shapes of found timber enabled improvisation: 'Driftwood is perfect for that. It gave you the latitude to make mistakes.' The critical leap into a professional career came after Wright travelled through Western Australia, and met woodworkers, such as Glen Holst in Bridgetown, who gave him a treasury of practical advice. Wright admits a talent for picking up skills through observation; he has never pursued any formal training in furniture making. In his view most available courses are focused on industrial design, rather than creative expression.

From driftwood, Wright began scrounging for recycled timber. The 1990s was a golden time for demolition in Victoria, with the state premier, Jeff Kennett, privatising utilities and selling off state buildings. For Wright, a key commitment to wood was occasioned by the demolition of the Repatriation Hospital in Bundoora. He spent $1000 on timber – 'money I didn't have'. The supply included jarrah bearers and was enough for two years' work.

During this period Wright became less interested in the recycled aesthetic and more concerned for the entire tree. He began to develop relationships with millers who would cut down a whole tree and cut it up to his specifications. Thus evolved the key to his craft – the patient business of listening to the materials in order to develop the best design. 'You get a tree and cut it open and fold it open, you don't know what it's going to be like. It unveils itself.' For a craftsperson, such uncertainty is both a hazard and a source of creative energy.

There is a broader historical dimension to the work of this artist. Wright sees the colonial skill inheritance as being based around European timbers. These timbers, such as mahogany, came from straight trees that were easily dried and easily shaped. The conventional wisdom about the perversity of Australian timbers was overstated. 'Greatest difficulty is imagination, because they can't bring themselves to imagine them as valuable, unique materials – just part of our inherent hostility to an Australian landscape. Part of that is conveniently to imagine that eucalypts are useless, same with acacias.' Within this mindset, Australian timber was seen as fit for firewood at the best. There was no avenue for appreciating its waywardness as a sign of beauty.

While Wright avoids shortcuts in making – you'd be hard-pressed to find a screw

Facing page:
Damien Wright
Black 2004
ancient redgum
190 x 75 x 75 cm
Photo: Gerard Warrener 'dpi'
Private collection

or nail in his joinery – his designs are modernist in their simplicity. Box-like forms provide generous linear surfaces. The timber is able to express itself undistracted by ornament. In the Federal Courts of Melbourne, Wright has introduced wallowa, gidgee and brigalow, ancient redgum and tiger myrtle. For the National Gallery of Victoria and Immigration Museum, Wright has uplifted ironbark. Many of these projects have involved collaborations with designers and architects that aspire to a mutual respect between maker and drawer.

Wright is deeply committed to reconciliation. He sees timber as a natural material of cultural understanding. *Black* is a privately commissioned sculpture made from petrified redgum hauled out of the Murray River. Ancient redgum is a particularly difficult timber to use. Once it is taken out of the water, it quickly loses moisture and begins to crack. Wright has found a way of working with this process as a source of creative expression; he has produced a monumental sculpture that is charged with energy. Wright describes the work as 'a melancholy, brooding piece that says something about the difficulty and struggle of coming to grips with the darkness that lies at the core of all human suffering. The result is graceful and optimistic, but it is not easy – just as it is not easy for any of us to reconcile the black heart of our own histories.' As though practising a kind of cultural alchemy, Wright hopes to find opportunities for moral transformation in the very material stuff of the land.

The Wright family has turned a complete circle with Damien's career. At a time when opportunities to effect political change seem elusive, the son has found a means to realise the family's radical nationalism in the realm of everyday life. Wright forces us to confront our image of central Australia as barren, and invites us to enjoy its beauty in the grain, texture and rich colours of the acacias. Years after following his father to the desert, Damien has now taught him woodwork and employs him part time in his workshop.

For Wright, furniture making is an immersive experience that returns him to the free spirit of his childhood. 'When I'm in the middle of it I'm the same person I was when I was ten, building a billycart or rabbit hutch or cubby-house, suit of armour or trampoline.' It seems the antithesis of the hallowed public realm where his work finds itself. Through his understanding of our core fibres, Wright brings this attitude of bush independence into our most authoritative spaces.

Damien Wright
Black (detail) 2004
ancient redgum
190 x 75 x 75 cm
Photo: Gerard Warrener 'dpi'
Private collection

Chapter 2: **F O S S I C K E R S**

While some artists gather materials from the land, others collect the materials for their art from the built environment. It would be expected of an artist to turn his or her back on the crass consumerism that typifies most Australian cities for the task of the artist is to offer an alternative to the degraded materialism of a disposable culture. But rather than refuse this culture, the artists featured here embrace the world of rubbish. They see the detritus of consumerism as an opportunity to recover a mystery of artistic creation.

Roseanne Bartley

In New Zealand the proximity of Maori and Pakeha populations is formalised in a policy of biculturalism. This policy is given artistic content in the attempts by those of European descent to identify as native New Zealanders. In the 1970s Pakeha figures such as the painter Colin McCahon, the historian Michael King and poet James Baxter admitted to the influence of Maori culture in their close relationship to the land.

Roseanne Bartley

The Pakeha sensibility has been particularly strong in jewellery, with many makers adopting Maori and Pacific Islander techniques and forms to develop an art that reflects their sense of place. In the late 1980s artists such as Alan Preston and Warwick Freeman fossicked for local materials – 'stone, bone and shell' – rather than work with more conventional diamonds and gold. Given the steady flow of New Zealanders to Australia, it is not surprising that this mentality has influenced the course of Australian craft.

So how might a New Zealander respond to urban Australia? For a jeweller from New Zealand this ancient continent is something far more alien. Rather than dig under pavements for local stone, Roseanne Bartley has uncovered what is authentically *inauthentic* in Australian life. How did she find herself across the ditch, and what did she find that could represent her new land?

It was partly an accident of birth. After growing up in Auckland, Bartley tried a number of 'practical' vocations, including primary school teaching, horticulture and even some equestrian sports. At night, she pursued her true interest: classes with a Maori who taught bone-carving. There she met up with an acquaintance, Margie Phillips, and found they shared a birthday. Phillips practiced bone-carving in her

Facing page:
Roseanne Bartley
Specimen 1997
typewriter keys, 925 silver
6 x 6 cm
Photo: Adi Lander

Roseanne Bartley
*Materialising the
Un-Australian* 2000
sterling silver, silk, brass
1 x 6 cm
Photo: Andrew Barcham

studio where Bartley started to develop her craft skills. She was then introduced to an American jeweller, Daniel Clasby, also born on the same day; he offered her space in his studio. At that time, in 1986, there were no formal courses for jewellery available in New Zealand. Clasby's workshops were open-ended, though his own work featured the use of text, which was to be a significant element in Bartley's repertoire. Eventually, his advice for Bartley was to go west, to Australia.

In 1988 Bartley enrolled in Gold and Silversmithing at the Royal Melbourne Institute of Technology, where she studied under leading jewellers Robert Baines, Carlier Makigawa and Marian Hosking. After graduating, she helped form the Independent Contemporary Jewellers group which sought exhibition opportunities outside of mainstream venues. Collective action was a familiar mode to a New Zealander; in Bartley's home country artists are often thrown on their own resources to make things happen.

Bartley started to explore Melbourne's markets for odd bits and pieces that she might incorporate into her work. She began using the tops of taps and old brushes – obsolete objects with interesting text or a history of wear on their surfaces.

The breakthrough came with her discovery of outmoded technology. In 1997 Bartley emerged as an exhibiting jeweller with *Homage to Qwerty* at Linden Gallery, Melbourne. This was a series of work using abandoned typewriters. Plastic letters were set like gems spelling out organic forms, and strikers formed flowers. The material emerged from an interest in word play and a love of visiting markets, where abandoned typewriters could then be bought cheaply. During this exhibition, Bartley also started using audience interaction. Messages left by visitors on a typewriter were used in the later *Body of Language* exhibition.

Finding herself settled in Australia, Bartley decided to officially change her nationality. Around this time, Australia was preparing itself for the Sydney Olympics, and there was some urgency to construct a national image for presentation to the world. Bartley found she could not relate to the popularist Australian emblems, such as Kylie surfing on a giant thong, dancing kangaroos or stockmen on horseback. Nor could she feel comfortable with the exclusionary zone that was emerging to define certain people as 'un-Australian', particularly asylum seekers.

Bartley decided that it was important to go outside the relatively passive gallery

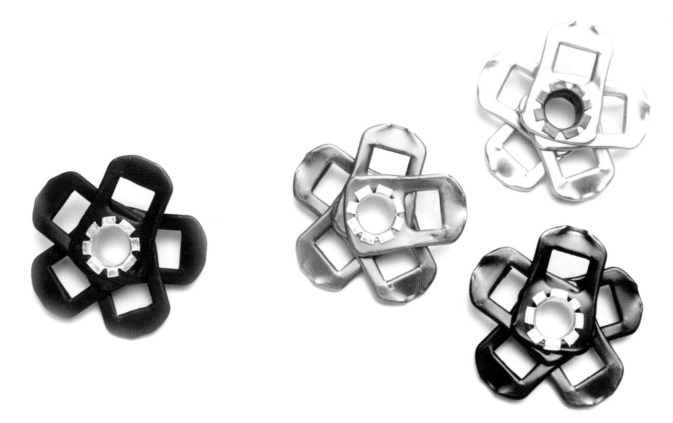

Roseanne Bartley
Found Out – Floral Brooches 2004
aluminium ring-pulls, stainless steel
each 3 cm diameter
Photo: Terence Bogue

setting and to engage visitors directly in an exhibition. She called for volunteers to enlist in an event called *Body of Language*, to be held on Australia Day, 2002. At an official ceremony, one hundred enlisted participants received silver tags bearing names they had nominated to describe their identities, including 'Un-Australian', 'Queue Jumper' or 'Digger'. As a 'distributed' exhibition, each participant carried his or her tag into the world over two weeks and recorded the responses of others to it. Many felt it liberating to actively own words that might otherwise be considered a slur on their identity.

Complementing this roaming event, a series of city venues displayed Bartley's work. She had rendered in fine silver some everyday objects whose iconic status as national symbols had not been recognised. 'I began to question, what are the things people use that signify to me what it means to be Australians.' The objects included a packet of cigarettes, a drink can and a take-away spoon with a fries packet. One Flinders Lane window showed a *'Sorry' Word Dispenser*, from which emerged a simple word that was considered at the time especially charged.

Bartley's next step was to seek out objects themselves and find ways of turning them into items of worth. It seemed important that she look to the immediate world at her feet. The distance between her home and the 7/11 convenience store at the corner is about as long it takes to eat an ice cream. As a result her front door step gathers a daily harvest of ice cream sticks. Bartley focused on the word printed on these – 'HEAVEN' – as a form of found text. While overseas, she sought out local varieties of ice cream stick Finding a large number of Magnum ice cream sticks in Italy, she produced a necklace titled *Magnum Opus*.

Bartley then ventured beyond her door step and visited a nearby park, which has a variety of sporting facilities including a golf range. She admits not to being interested in the sporting activity itself – more what gets left behind. She has set into brooches seemingly worthless items such as perished tennis and golf balls. These works evoke the Japanese idea of *sabi*, which celebrates the patina of decay on exposed objects. The degraded nature of Bartley's relics elevates objects beyond their status as consumables.

The phrase 'Nothing is sacred' is commonly used to describe the rebellious nature of modern artists, but in the case of Bartley is the reverse applies. 'Nothing is profane' for this jeweller, eager to celebrate the most mundane objects as forms of adornment. Rosettes made from drink can tops are being marketed in a jewellery range labelled *Found Out*.

Bartley maintains an intellectual involvement in her homeland. Through articles and reviews, she is an active commentator on New Zealand cultural affairs. A new generation of jewellers shares her fossicking mentality. The Auckland jeweller Pauline Bern has created a series of work utilising fragments of shells from the beach that are repaired with thread. These works speak for a gentle intervention into the fraught politics of land and sea in bicultural New Zealand.

Bartley elevates the lowest of the low. She transforms the crud of consumerism into a precious ornament for the body. She has translated the New Zealand consciousness of place to Australia, and in so doing changed our focus from natural materials to consumer packaging. She prompts us to think about authentic identity in the most inauthentic products. And along the way, Bartley renews the mission of jewellery to create objects of beauty.

Roseanne Bartley
A packet of cigarettes, a takeaway spoon and a drink can with heritage table card 2002
950 silver
variable dimensions
Photo: Terence Bogue

Lorraine Connelly-Northey

Lorraine Connelly-Northey

Lorraine Connelly-Northey
Dilly Bag 2002
wire mesh, wire, synthetic
polymer paint
57 x 40 x 7 cm

Aboriginal contemporary craft is often overlooked. The late twentieth century saw the recognition of Aboriginal painting on both the national and world stages. Large canvases were heralded for both their formal beauty and enduring cultural meaning. Off-stage were the Aboriginal crafts which predate painting, the objects such as coolamons and dilly bags.

There have been moments when Aboriginal craft has found recognition beyond the purely ethnographic collections in museums. The 1997 Venice Biennale included work by the Ngarrindjeri weaver Yvonne Koolmatrie, who produced sculptures from eel trap forms using traditional basket-making techniques. Exhibited alongside Koolmatrie was Emily Kngwarreye, who often worked in batik. Exhibitions of Hermannsburg pottery or Arnhem Land jewellery continue to appear at times, but these events are sporadic.

Craft might seem irrelevant to urbanised Aboriginal communities, such as the Koori in south-eastern Australia, who don't always have the experience of traditional craft to fall back on. The paths of artists within such communities must of necessity be more individual. One artist who has found her own way through craft is Lorraine Connelly-Northey. She powerfully evokes the cultural traditions of her ancestors while finding her own individual means of creation. Rather than copying traditional artefacts as they might be found in museums, Connelly-Northey sets out to re-create Aboriginal culture in ways that are true to her own world. Hers is a remarkable story of dedication to learning outside formal education.

From the age of seventeen, Connelly-Northey had worked as a public servant in Melbourne. She had had positions in various Aboriginal Affairs portfolios. After ten years of service, she decided to retrace her roots, asking herself, 'Where to now, as a young woman of Aboriginal descent?'

She remembered her own childhood, growing up along the Murray River and in the Mallee district – one in a family of six children. Her Aboriginal mother was descended from the Waradgerie people and her father was from Irish stock. Her mother's father was Alfred Knocker Williams, a naïve artist who signed his work 'Made in Australia by Wongibong, Waradgerie tribe'. The childhood home was a typical scene of rural self-reliance: her mother crocheted wool and wove pine needles into objects of use.

To give her mother a break, Lorraine's father used to take the children out bush 'to live off the land'. He introduced them to bush life, bush craft and the Aboriginal ways. In particular, he taught them about the various bush environments; the waterways; the animals and plants, and their usage. Lorraine remembers rabbit-trapping, yabbying, catching redfin, and the annual collection and engorgement on sweet quandong in the Mallee. Following his own cultural priorities, her Irish father accompanied every meal with potatoes. While fishing at the river Lorraine was introduced to the kumbungi (now spelt 'cumbungi') plant and learnt how to weave the leaves for matting. 'Dad used to pick that from the river and cart that over the Mallee for us to weave and play with. We used to plait them in and out and make mats to sit on.' She used these flotation devices for carrying gathered mussels, similar to traditional Aboriginal ways of using kumbungi mats.

Connelly-Northey aspired to be as good an artist as Yvonne Koolmatrie, but using materials from her own country. To do this, she realised that she needed to go back to the source, physically. So she resigned from her job, left her husband in Adelaide, and with a child in tow returned to Swan Hill to rediscover the world of her childhood.

Although Connelly-Northey was born and bred in the area, she is a Waradgerie descendent and was therefore uncomfortable about her access to traditional sources in the Wamba Wamba and Wadi Wadi countries. However, she was not satisfied just to weave the locally reputable grasses and sedges. She knew she needed to rediscover her childhood environments for inspiration in her work.

Connelly-Northey resided in her parental home for five years, and explored the bush with her father and son almost everyday. Having been a 'man of the land' most of his life, her father was able to hand on further knowledge about the river and its tributaries, telling her about the natural water sumps of the Mallee and explaining the network of channels and dams. He also showed her how to read the clouds and forecast weather; he pointed out different soil types and good camping spots; he introduced her to local animals, their habitats and behaviours, and to numerous plants, both native and introduced.

It was a process of renewal. Connelly-Northey's father helped her rediscover the stands of sweet quandongs she had feasted on as a child, thirty years previously. Her son could now experience the distinctive taste of the fruit and lay down his own mem-

Lorraine Connelly-Northey
Detail of installation from exhibition
Narrbangs, Swan Hill Regional Art
Gallery, October 2004
Photo: Mick Cullin

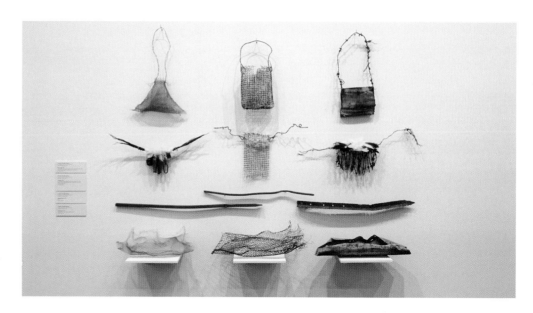

Lorraine Connelly-Northey
Installation from RAKA Award 2004
Ian Potter Museum of Art, the
University of Melbourne

ories. And so a lost world of the quandong was re-discovered. Back home the quandongs were shared, preserved or made into conserve. Her son played marbles with quandong nuts found under the trees, while Connelly-Northey rolled them under her feet as a massage. The family prepared the nuts in order to grow new plants, and kernels were eaten raw as practised by the Aboriginal communities from Robinvale. Oil was extracted and used as a scalp rub similar in the manner of central Australian Aborigines. Connelly-Northey explored the fresh plant further for its weaving uses – she soaked, boiled, crushed, dried, dyed and dye-extracted the plant. Other plants were also collected, their locations mapped and photographs developed. Thus Connelly-Northey continued to accrue her knowledge of the area.

Learning from her father where to find materials was one thing. What should she do with them? Connelly-Northey decided to research weaving techniques at the local library. With her expanding knowledge, she became involved in the Aboriginal Education Program. 'I've got no education behind me. It's just what I've begged, borrowed and stolen.' For this artist, learning is a continuing process. In 1996 the then director of the Swan Hill Regional Gallery, Linda Lucas, helped Connelly-Northey to organise a workshop with Yvonne Koolmatrie. The latter was so impressed with Connelly-Northey's first attempts to weave that she nominated her 'the weaver of the class'.

In the late 1990s Connelly-Northey began to seek out found materials. She started with corrugated iron, typical of her father's heritage, which she painted with acrylic paints in Aboriginal designs, to represent her mother's background. After a while she was no longer prepared to invest the time it took to paint; she instead rubbed down the iron with ochre. Sensing something was lacking, Connelly-Northey attempted to reshape the already corrugated material. 'When I see all these things lying around that don't belong, like old rubbish tips, I think that I can make something – they're just there. How could I utilise them, but stay on the same track that I'm on?'

Her knowledge of traditional Aboriginal society, especially of tools and implements used, helped her realise that she had reshaped this piece of iron into a coolamon, a basin-shaped dished used traditionally by Aboriginal gatherers to collect food. This discovery meant that, with her knowledge of weaving techniques, Connelly-Northey could collect found pieces that closely represented what a finished product of weaving might look like. She could take a piece of mesh or coiled wire, and reshape it to make a dilly bag without taking fibre from the bush.

So she began to appropriate found pieces of metal – old springs, fencing wire, mesh, motor parts, and so on. An opportunity for experimentation came when her father's friend pulled down a cattleyard that his father had built some fifty years prior. Says Connelly-Northey, 'The cocky will use a machine that pushes the fence down, which releases chook wire and comes in the beautiful coiling shape. I've coiled it into matting.' She burnt the timber, iron and wires for different lengths of time to achieve various colours and textures. In the meantime, someone dropped off five hundred horseshoes, which she made into a large metal cod fish. Anything was eligible for art, with enough imagination.

Part of the process for Connelly-Northey is determining how to treat the found metal. Once she shaped a coolamon out of an old windmill blade. Sometimes she will decide to alter the colour of a piece of metal by heating it.

Connelly-Northey is boundlessly creative , despite many responsibilities to family and community (she refuses to have a phone), For the 2004 RAKA award, she fashioned traditional Aboriginal artefacts out of found materials. The lap-lap was made from iron springs, pelican feathers and wire cable. Coolamons were made from wire mesh. The same year in Swan Hill, she created an installation of one hundred dilly bags. From a miscellany of rusted wire and rural debris, she made a bounty of traditional artefacts.

Connelly-Northey may one day feel authorised to use natural fibres and so weave sublime objects the way her mentor Yvonne Koolmatrie does. But in the meantime, this artist is able to take a poetic levy from what does not belong in her land. In so doing she reconstructs a precious cultural cargo from the detritus of colonisation.

Paull McKee

Most textile artists are women. Domestic crafts are resurgent and women can be found knitting in nightclubs. Is there a place for men in the renaissance of domestic crafts? Paull McKee has reached a point where he can pursue the textile arts he loves, while being true to his gender. McKee's position reflects the soft heart of Australian male nationalism, the realm of swags, blueys and waggas. Getting there was a long journey.

McKee was born in Perth of Irish colonial heritage. Relatives on his mother's side arrived as convicts, while those on his father's side settled around Ballarat. Colour, for McKee, is a matter of identity. As he explains in simple terms, 'I'm White.' Paull grew up in the small town of Kojonup in the farming district of south-west Australia; his parents ran the local newsagency. Looking back he recognises the contradiction between the poverty of inhabitants in the town and the prosperity of the region. Townspeople were mostly 'slave labour for [the] surrounding farm district'. As McKee reflects, 'We were working class – then there were the bank managers and cockies.' This class difference has underpinned the artist's course in life, laying down the parameters of his creative struggle.

McKee remembers growing up in the 1970s, before television, when craft was a way of life. He recalls an interest in art beginning at kindergarten, when he noticed how much attention he could get for doing a picture.

Like many boys of his generation, Paul was trained in metal and wood work. However, he was more attracted to sewing, as he explains, 'because I was told not to … Boys don't sew.' It was unpicking his mother's and sister's sewing that initiated him into textiles. 'I was allowed to unpick the hems that were wrong.' He developed close relations with women neighbours who embodied the culture of the Country Women's Association. There were a number of 'clandestine textile moments', as McKee recalls. 'Nana Thornbury made pot holders on her treadle machine. Mrs Sullivan, who taught me about local flora and gardening in general, was also a great crocheter.'

Paull McKee at work

Facing page:
Paull McKee
Inside Out 2001
collected old suit jacket
multiple dimensions

Paull McKee
Untitled Wagga Diptych 2001
collected wool blankets, heat
pressed, wool thread, hessian back
106 x 106, 106 x 78 cm

Meanwhile he worked in an abattoir to earn some pocket money. McKee describes his creative interests as a 'life jacket to keep me afloat within a classist society that doesn't expect much from working class men'. [13]

McKee studied textile design at the Western Australian Institute of Technology (then known as WAIT; now Curtin University) and started work in pattern cutting. Realising that he needed to work things out for himself, he learned how to pour beers and took himself on a working tour around Australia. McKee ended up in Adelaide and enrolled in Art and Design at the University of South Australia, where he discovered the wild insights of post-structuralist theory, including deconstruction and queer theory. He sees this experience as enabling him to identify as gay and place his own marginalisation in a broader picture: 'The positioning of gay oppression is central to men's oppression.' Much of this gender theory he had to invent himself as he could find nothing for men that was equivalent to the feminist movement.

McKee then he moved to the Canberra School of Art, where he began to give form to his art. He returned to sewing and made an installation based on his childhood nickname, Pansy. But rather than celebrate his difference from the mainstream, McKee was committed to identifying his personal struggle with a popular cause. He went to the heart of Australian male nationalism to recover its own textile traditions.

And so McKee discovered the Australian tradition of the wagga (also known as the 'wogger', 'bush quilt', 'utility rug' or 'bush rug'). Waggas were originally made in the late nineteenth century from hessian backed by calico bags from the Wagga Wagga Flour Mill. McKee comments that the story of the wagga 'belongs to the story of the swag and bluey. It's intrinsic to the story of masculinity in Australia.' For McKee, the task was to transform the wagga from a nostalgic museum item to a medium of expression in contemporary craft.

The title of his exhibition of waggas in 2002 was *Idea of Perfection*, taken from the novel by Kate Grenville. In Grenville's story the residents of a typical small Australian town, Karakarook, decide to establish a museum of ordinary things made by people without the money to purchase goods from shops. The novel evokes the modest world of country crafts: 'There was a rocking-chair draped with crocheted blankets, and shelves of jams, and face-washers with KARAKAROOK NSW done by hand in cross-stitch in the corner.'[14] This is the warm heart of Australian make-do culture that McKee seeks to acknowledge.

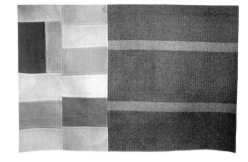

Paull McKee
Wagga: V554 1943 I
collected wool blankets, eucalyptus dyes, heat-pressed, hessian back
87 x 134 cm

The charm of the wagga partly lies in the catholic use of materials. Whatever came to hand could be incorporated, including sugar bags, old blankets, and scraps of clothing. McKee used this freedom to develop abstract works which used materials for visual effect. His waggas incorporated old shirts, Hessian bags and disused blankets.

As well as making work based on waggas, McKee is concerned to change the way we look at these objects. Rather than adopting a purely technical definition, McKee argues that waggas should be understood as part of our culture of necessity. It's not a matter of craftsmanship; he says, 'I like that make-do culture shows its seams, has wonky sewing and never a straight line'.[15]

He is keen that folk craft stays true to its origins. According to McKee, 'The greatest strengths of make-do culture lie in its warmth, hope and humour.' He argues that institutional recognition, while deserved, risks coopting a folk tradition into professional agendas. And he is therefore against the process of sanitisation that accompanies the incorporation of folk craft into the museum. For McKee, craft still needs to be a living art, 'an act of giving ... an act of intelligence, a human act, an act of hope'.

As an artist, McKee goes beyond simply acknowledging folk culture. In his history of American art, *American Visions*, Robert Hughes ordains the Amish quilts from Lancaster as the first great works of modernist abstraction, predating the canvases of

Facing page:
Sally Marsland
Why are you like this and not like that? 2004
1st row, l–r: epoxy resin cast copy of a Wedgwood cup; lathe-turned and anodised aluminium; epoxy resin, mixed with powdered pigment and poured into mould constructed from plastic sheet and sticky tape.
2nd row, l–r: found wooden bowl, partially saw-cut and painted; epoxy resin, poured into a plastic cup, Paulonia offcut.
3rd row, l–r: raised and anodised aluminium (1994), epoxy resin, mixed with powdered pigment, poured into sticky-tape mould and then lathe-turned; paint layers painted onto cast wax copy of found ceramic jug then wax melted away.
Vessels 50–150mm high
4th row, l–r: English ash, lathe-turned and constructed copy of a found ceramic jug; 925 silver, cast from wax and plastic spoons (1999); epoxy resin (mixed with powdered pigment) cast copy of a Guy Boyd ramekin.
Photo: Julian Hutchens

Sally Marsland in her studio
Photo: Stephen Bram

Rothko. While McKee would not arrogate the title of abstract painter, he highlights the formal beauty of the wagga, beyond either its utility as a textile or its role as a historical artefact. He uses the device of the diptych to distance our eyes from the practical role of the blankets. In doing this he makes the humble scraps of fabric valuable twice over – first as objects of comfort, and second as works of beauty.

McKee pursued this further in a majestic work for the 2005 Tamworth Fibre Textile Biennial. In *Bequeathed* he added to his signature materials the element of colour. Eucalyptus dyes lent his work a pictorial boldness that both honoured the origin of the artist's materials and made a creative difference through colour.

McKee continues his investigations into male textile traditions with works that explore the tradition of bush tailor. His piece *Inside Out* features a jacket that has been cobbled together from old outmoded suits.

McKee's identity as working-class gay offers him a distance from mainstream culture. Through his textile work, McKee has found his own path back to that common centre. His work celebrates an extremely rare form of commonness, a form that McKee has made his own. The results are redemptive works of subtle beauty.

Sally Marsland

Sally Marsland's work bench is a parliament of things. There are objects from all corners of life. Marsland's craft is to develop a constitution in which these things have a voice of their own. She fashions deliberately minimal concepts that bring together a maximum of things. Marsland introduces a formalism into the business of making the common precious.

Marsland grew up in the Victorian high country. Her parents were teachers who worked in Bogong and Mount Beauty, both small towns. After school Marsland initially enrolled in an architecture course, to fulfil a childhood ambition. She soon found that this did not allow much creative expression. Taking some time off during her course, she worked with jeweller Viliama Grakalic; she built up her folio and was subsequently admitted to the prestigious Gold and Silversmithing course at the Royal Melbourne Institute of Technology (RMIT).

Marsland began her artistic practice far from traditional jewellery. Her first exhibited work, for a show titled *Pursued Realities* (1994), curated by Simone le Amon), included four vitrines, each containing a multitude of objects collected from the back

Sally Marsland
*Studio Table (*detail) 1995
including completed salt shakers (2nd,
3rd, 5th, 6th and 7th from left: anodised
aluminium, stainless steel, 925 silver),
pepper grinders (1st and 4th from left:
925 silver, aluminium, steel), works
in progress, paper models, found objects
Photo: Sally Marsland

of friends' cupboards. This was a bold move; it signalled a non-hierarchical attitude to craft that would continue to surface in following exhibitions.

Marsland was immediately attracted to the lathe as a creative instrument. 'It's very reductive – you remove material.' Her first major exhibition realised the potential of the lathe as a creative tool. *A Group of Juicy Green Protrusions* (with Nicholas Bastin, 1997) featured a multitude of cylindrical objects. The profusion of pieces resisted the viewer's expectations of the precious object, and reflected the scene in an opportunity shop more than an art gallery.

In 1998 Marsland went to the Akademie der Bildenden Künste in Munich to study with Swiss jeweller Otto Künzli. Künzli's reductive approach to ornamentation has helped spawn a thriving European engagement in conceptual jewellery, evident in Amsterdam's Galerie Ra. The influence of Künzli is also to be experienced at Melbourne's Gallery Funaki. Marsland found her time in Germany a particularly intensive period – 'people sleeping in their studios'. At this time she discovered the importance of 'opening out' materials.

While overseas Marsland also started using paint. She had been impressed by the story of a boat that had been painted so many times it sank when it was stripped back. She firstly painted balloons, coating them with enough layers of paint to create a solid object. She then progressed to other objects. 'So I just got a jug from a flea market ... then made a rubber mould, then a wax copy, then painted onto the outside of the wax, then melted the wax back.' Marsland had developed a technique that was like producing a three-dimensional shadowgram. The resulting husk bore a direct imprint of the original object. Through this method, Marsland could now play with colour, while allowing the things themselves to determine the form. Her process laid the ground for a powerful series of exhibitions back in Melbourne at Galleri Funaki.

The idea for a new body of work came one day when she was mixing graphic pigment with car filler. Marsland noticed that the mixture was the same colour as oxidised silver – almost black. She began to consider other objects around her that shared this colour, including stick-on magnets, slate and bicycle tube. From this emerged a series of brooches that incorporated found, fabricated and cast objects. *Almost Black* (2000) featured a seemingly random assortment of things. The materials included oxidised 925 silver (cast from wax poured into a mould taken of an aluminium jelly cup), king william pine coloured with ink, paulownia (Chinese tree) dyed with textile dye,

Sally Marsland
Almost Black Brooches 2002
clockwise l–r: slate, oxidized silver, King William pine coloured with ink, Paulonia dyed with textile dye, car filler mixed with powdered graphite, epoxy resin mixed with powdered graphite.
centre: bone dyed with textile dye.
Photo: Sally Marsland

polyester resin mixed with graphite (pressed onto wax copies of two spoons joined together), epoxy resin mixed with graphite, slate and osso bucco bone dyed with textile dye, silver, pearls, a carbon fibre ski sock, bicycle tube, shirring elastic, and cotton darning thread.

The catalogue essay for *Almost Black* suggested that the work evoked a metaphysical engagement between being and nothingness. Black in its pure sense is nothing but nothing:

> Uninterrupted black, monotone, does to the visible what fur does for the audible. It muffles, cloaks, flattens an object, creates almost silhouettes of things.
> Almost provides some space that allows for life to occur.
> Almost is most alive when very, very close to its object. Almost is the difference between the part that is and the part that is not yet.

First-time visitors to a Sally Marsland exhibition are likely to be disconcerted. An exhibition such as *Almost Black* seems initially little more than a random collection of charred things – something quite incongruous on the pristine white shelves of a chic Melbourne gallery. It takes a while for the connections between objects to develop.

The concept driving *Almost Black* operated like a casual dress code in which even the most humble of objects had a place. Marsland's next exhibition was the symmetrical obverse. *Flat Colour* (2002) was a technicolour exhibition with no objects other than those made by the artist. Marsland's method was devastatingly simple. As she described it, 'The process is almost exactly like icing in that the more powder you add to the resin the thicker it gets.' After mixing pigment with epoxy resin, Marsland would apply a blob of the mixture onto an acrylic sheet with a spatula. Once it had thoroughly cured, after several days, she would then decide what colour, if any, needed to be added next. Brooch fittings were inserted into the substance just before it set.

The flat colour brooches are the expression of contradictory intentions. On the one hand, Marsland tries to avoid self-conscious intervention and instead allows for random expressions of colour. But on the other hand, she has to make very deliberate choices about the kind of colour to use. 'I don't want to be responsible about choices, but I'm a control freak.' Marsland is not necessarily comfortable with her level of deliberation – 'I didn't want them to be drawings.' It is this kind of tension that engages viewers.

The following exhibition returned to the poetry of things. *Why Are You Like This and Not Like That?* (2004) combined the intentions behind both previous exhibitions: it featured colour and found objects. For this exhibition Marsland chose objects without any regard to their official value. She selected objects to hand – whatever expressed something interesting about the state of being a vessel.

For each object Marsland determined the most appropriate creative intervention. In the case of a ceramic pot she made herself when only twelve years old, no intervention was necessary. Yet a ceramic bottle was painstakingly turned in aluminium. Tin cans were simply powder-coated a different colour. A ceramic cup was turned in wood by an ex-teacher. Other vessels were cast in brightly coloured resin using different methods. Some objects were lathed, some were cast, some were fabricated from memory, and some were just as they are.

What mattered was not the specific material or form, but individual responses to specific objects in relation to one another. Marsland's choices were informed by the way things sat together. Each object could respond to the underlying question: 'Why are you like this and not like that?'

The 2004 exhibition realised a further evolution of mould making. While visiting family back in Myrtleford, Marsland passsed time by setting up a table to cast objects from the local opportunity shop. 'I bought a couple of things, looked at them for ages. I cut away the bits that I thought didn't need to be there.' There was no attempt from Marsland to justify her interventions as craft. As viewers, we were called to witness the objects as they stood before us. How well they fitted in to conventional notions of craft was irrelevant. As writer Alex Selenitsch noted, 'They were vessels where the contents were beginning to take over and become the object.'[16]

It is not easy to reduce Marsland's work to a single theme. In talking about what drives her, the artist admits to a restless creativity: 'The cells in your body can't sit still.' There's also the glory: 'You want to make something beautiful so people can like you.' But she admits that the most important 'ingredient' is 'to be honest'. This means allowing the materials to speak for themselves.

Sally Marsland
Flat Colour Brooches 2002
epoxy resin mixed with powdered pigment
variable dimensions
Photo: Terence Bogue

For materials to speak for themselves, certain voices must remain quiet. Marsland refuses to overlay her work with too much language. Her titles are descriptive. 'We're so word-based, that it's easier – that language muscle as compared to the visual muscle. We've privileged words.' Hers is a yoga-like craft that seeks to go beyond routine patterns of meaning.

Minimal titles enable an experimental approach. Marsland identifies with the practice of musicians such as Brian Eno, whose work involves programming processes where the result cannot be controlled. Eno advocates 'a point of discipline to accept this passive role, and, for once, to ignore the tendency to play artist by dabbling and interfering'.[17]

So for Marsland exhibition titles are like hypotheses. Her experimental method draws on whatever materials or techniques are necessary to give body to the meaning of the title. She is not interested in championing the lowly object per se. Marsland is more interested in the poetry of things. For her, an old bone has as much poetry as a diamond ring – or more.

Fleur Schell

In her account of the re-invention of porcelain in eighteenth-century Europe, Janet Gleeson evokes the wonder with which porcelain was first apprehended.

> As glossy as the richly coloured silks with which the ships were laden, as flawlessly white as the spray which broke over their bows on their long treacherous journeys, this magical substance was so eggshell fine that you could hold it to the sun and see daylight through it, so perfect that if you tapped it a musical note would resound.[18]

Gleeson describes how 'china mania' captivated the aristocracy of Europe in the eighteenth century. In cities such as Dresden and Delft craftsmen fabricated extraordinary porcelain objects that became potent symbols of prestige.

In Australia a version of this tradition persisted up to the 1960s: 'respectable' homes featured a cabinet of precious china, never to be used. But porcelain has little place in modern homes where functionality outweighs ornament. While porcelain seems no longer to play a major decorative role, a West Australian ceramicist has been able to discover new dimensions of its musical power. The story is like a fairy tale.

Fleur Schell grew up on a farm 130 kilometres north-east of Perth. The property had been owned by the family for six generations. The first Australian Schell migrated from Germany and helped build the railway line between Perth and Kalgoorlie.

Fleur Schell

Fleur Schell

Sound Funnel: infundibular series 2002
porcelain, fabric, metal, plastic
68 x 31 cm

Fleur Schell
Production Line 2000
porcelain, mixed media
110 x 52 cm

Fleur Schell
Temporal Sounds (detail) 1999
fine china, mixed media

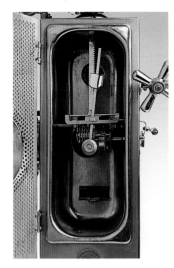

Along the way he found land that he thought would be good for making wine. There soon began to appear oats, canola, barley, merino sheep, and Angus cows.

Fatefully, the property happened to be adjacent to one of the richest kaolin deposits in the world. The clay pit subsequently supplied Australian Bone China, which had its kilns in Subiaco, Perth. Throughout her childhood, Fleur enjoyed the boundless possibilities of clay. 'When I was a little girl, I used to get on my motorbike and go out to a dam on our farm that had pure kaolin. And I used to make tea sets on the sides of the dam.' Schell fell in love with porcelain – 'It was so pure, and the sensation of squeezing it through your fingers and toes was so seductive.' These childhood pleasures were to become a rich inheritance.

Schell's path into the world was not straight. There were no ceramicists in her family. Her mother was a music teacher who encouraged her daughter to play flute. In the end, Schell chose to pursue visual arts. But it was through porcelain that she was able to unite the visual with music.

Schell is attracted to the way the Chinese defined porcelain by the sound it made when struck. One of her early works consisted of porcelain copies of bottles that had been kept by her family over many generations, and recycled as bells and percussion instruments.

Before Schell was able to return to porcelain she gained a solid skill base in ceramics. She completed a diploma at the Western Australian School of Art and Design which taught her basic techniques in throwing. She graduated to Sculpture at Curtin University, and then studied industrial mould making with Penny Smith in Hobart. She returned to Curtin to teach, and was then offered an invitation to spend a year at the Alberta College of Art and Design in Canada.

The idea of making musical instruments came to Schell one day at a shopping centre when a child approached her with a sliding lolly whistle. This prompted her to think of mechanical devices that slide – 'the form was dictated by the action of the sound'. Most of Schell's instruments are bag-pipe in form. They include tubes and bladders. For Schell, the conjunction of hard porcelain with velvet is particularly effective.

True to her childhood experience, Schell today uses Australian Bone China; it is hospital grade and resists chipping, which is important when the work contains moving parts. To prevent porcelain meeting porcelain, Schell introduces a cartilage-like substance such as cork or resin, usually disguised. Fabric also forms an important part of her work; it is used for the cushions on which her objects rest. Usually lush velvet, the cushions reflect the quality of material lining an instrument case.

Schell divides artists into two groups: the makers for whom colour is an afterthought and the decorators who are more interested in the final appearance. She identifies with the former. Schell is drawn to the Art Deco era: 'There's a sense of freedom: they threw ergonomics out the window.' But her craftsmanship is baroque, and in style Schell is the opposite of a modernist artist such as Sally Marsland. Yet ideologically both artists share a modest sensibility toward things. For Schell, it is very important that viewers get the chance to handle and play her instruments.

Fleur Schell is particularly attracted to the humbleness of clay: 'From the moment you've put your finger into a ball of clay, you've created a vessel of some sort. It's a natural thing that we want to do.' Besides manipulating clay, much of Schell's time is spent finding recycled materials such as toasters and car parts that can be incorporated into her works.

Schell fashions highly idiosyncratic porcelain instruments of baroque complexity. Despite their extravagant appearance, they can be easily traced back to their humble origins – in the clay pit and junk heap.

Fleur Schell
Clariphone 1997
porcelain, mixed media
60 x 45 cm

Chapter 3: GLEANERS

Like the makers discussed previously, the artists in this chapter also deal with things that get left behind. But their interest is not in obsolescence. They are concerned instead with packaging. The ritual of consumption inevitably involves the destruction of ephemeral material: an object's packaging enables the process of unwrapping that grants its contents an aura. Artists Nicole Lister and David Herbert subvert this process by bestowing the substance of a commodity to the packaging itself.

Nicole Lister

The late Jacques Derrida promoted the philosophical method of deconstruction in the English-speaking world. While dazzling in its conceptual paradoxes, deconstruction can be applied to aesthetic practice quite simply. Following the dialectical principle that something *is* by virtue of what it *is not*, deconstruction brings to the fore what seems inessential in our world. In the case of art it searches out the supplement that sustains a work, such as the frame that surrounds a painting.

As a conceptual exercise, deconstruction is not often applied to material arts such as craft. However, in the case of the 'poor craft' discussed here the maker's attention moves to the element that supports the world of precious things – packaging. Supported by an environmentalist consciousness of waste, makers transform what we consider ephemeral into something of intrinsic beauty.

The Sydney ceramicist Nicole Lister has taken packaging to its most precious limit. She creates works of enduring beauty out of what is normally thrown away. To get there, she takes a detour through textiles.

In 1999 Lister received a New Work grant from the Australia Council. She began to explore the connection between ceramics and textiles, 'seeking to marry textile/dressmaking construction techniques (for example, pinning, tucking, pleating, folding, dyeing) with the ceramic material'. As handmade quilts from recycled materials can extend the life of fabrics, so Lister was interested in making porcelain 'quilts' and ceramic vessels from the remnants of a throwaway culture.

In an exhibition titled *Material Deceptions* (2001) at Sydney's Object Galleries Lister exhibited a series of exquisite ceramic pieces cast from cardboard and paper moulds. The work *Wrapping Cloth* rendered into porcelain the corrugated cardboard that is

Nicole Lister in her studio
Photo: Grant Ayre

Facing page:
Nicole Lister
Stacks of Work 2003
limoges porcelain, clear glaze interior
20 x 40 x 40 cm
Photo: Michel Brouet

Nicole Lister

Wrapping Cloth 2001

limoges porcelain, paperclay

11 x 75 x 75 cm

Collection: Museum of Modern Ceramic Art, Gifu

Photo: Michel Brouet

usually used to wrap precious ceramics. Of no value in itself, packaging, this servant of craft, is granted immortality as art. As viewers, we are able to still the world and consider the beauty of this form, the rhythm of corrugations, the looseness of fold, and the trace of the original object.

Lister's casting technique tells an interesting story. Given the delicate nature of cardboard, the artist chooses not to create a negative mould for her pieces. After some research, she has developed a claybody that she can paint in multiple layers onto cardboard moulds. The combustible material burns away during the firing process, leaving its other enduring self. This means that each piece is unique – requiring its own mould. This is a method that industry cannot copy.

Lister took the name 'wrapping cloth' from the Japanese expression for the cloth material used to encase food. Textiles provided inspiration for other works in the exhibition. *Precious Little Cover* (Powerhouse Museum, 1999) was inspired by Korean textiles from the Chosun Dynasty. Lister's interest in textiles reaches back to her childhood.

Lister comes from a practical family. Her mother worked as a machinist for the clothing company Berlei, and her father is a carpenter. She grew up in Sydney in the suburb of Rydalmere, and attended Macarthur Girls' High School in Parramatta.

She was encouraged by high school teachers to continue in ceramics and went on to complete a Bachelor of Education at the City Art Institute in 1988. For the next six years she taught visual arts in Australia and the United Kingdom. In 1994 Lister commenced part-time study in ceramics at Meadowbank TAFE; she completed an Advanced Diploma in Ceramics at East Sydney TAFE in 1997. During a ceramics conference in 1996, she worked as an assistant to the Czech ceramicist Jindra Vikova, who introduced her to the use of porcelain slip.

Lister's statement for the group show *Small* (1998), her first show after graduation, expresses her opposition to 'a system which denies its origins in the human making process and highlights the machine as maker – absorbing craft knowledge and skill, automatising it and redistributing it to unskilled workers'. It is disposable culture and the 'loss of individual expression' which she chooses to combat in her ceramic work. Her contribution to this exhibition, *Production Line*, consisted of a tower of cups, ironically bestowing monumentality on to what is otherwise of fleeting value.

Nicole Lister
Precious Little Cover (detail) 2001
limoges porcelain, paperclay,
onglaze decals
Photo: Michel Brouet

Nicole Lister
French Vanilla 2002
limoges porcelain
15 x 20 x 20 cm
Photo: Michel Brouet

The following year, her exhibition *No Picnic: Contemporary Porcelain* (Mura Clay Gallery) featured disposable containers made of porcelain – patty pans, paper plates and drinking cups. The piece *Stacks of Work* included a profusion of forms based on disposable cups.

Lister's recent work *A Convenient Arrangement* (2004) is comprised of slip-cast and hand-built components (coiled and pinched). Colour is introduced as an important element. What seems to be emerging in the artist's work is a formalism that expresses the essential beauty of simple shape and colour. As in the work of Sally Marsland, this formalism provides a democratic basis upon which the common might find a place for itself alongside the precious.

Lister is one of a generation of committed craftspersons who seek to champion their tradition by stepping outside it. In so doing she introduces free energy into the ceramic scene and makes work that is relevant to manic times.

David Herbert

David Herbert in his studio

Like a set of Matryoshka dolls, the consumable world is comprised of layers that never quite make it on their own. Think of the layers involved in acquiring a new television: cardboard box, Styrofoam, plastic sleeve and finally television, which is itself only a conduit for images from elsewhere, often promoting other objects that promise more possibilities. This continual deferment of consumerism can have a corrosive effect. All the more striking, then, that an artist such as David Herbert can make sublime objects based on the most ephemeral substance of our age.

Herbert's background is out of the ordinary. He started life in the small country town of Timboon in western Victoria. His parents were Baptist missionaries who moved to Indonesia when David was one year old. Herbert remembers enjoying the plethora of discarded objects where they were living – 'Nothing like Asia for that'. At the age of five, he went to school in the Cameron Highlands of Malaysia – 'A great place for rubbish'. He particularly liked scavenging around the old army barracks. Herbert eventually returned to Melbourne for high school, at the age of twelve, but he retained a love of discarded things.

Beachcombing has been an enduring source of discovery. And he remains particularly attracted to found pieces of old glass. As well as the forms themselves, he is interested in the history of the pieces. As he says, 'They are worn pieces and you wonder

David Herbert
Aperture 2005
lead crystal
21 x 49 x 14 cm
Photo: David McArthur

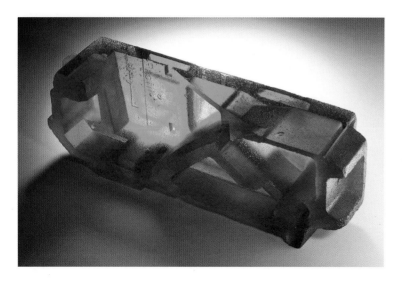

Above left:
David Herbert
Portal 2003
cast lead crystal
27 x 33 x 15 cm
Photo: David McArthur

Above right:
David Herbert
Overpass 2003
cast lead crystal
19 x 58 x 15 cm
Photo: David McArthur

where [they're] from.' Today Herbert makes his own glass out of objects washed up on city streets.

After studying at TAFE and the Royal Melbourne Institute of Technology, Herbert attended Monash University at Caulfield. Initially he studied ceramics there, but soon transferred into glass. He found that the wheelwork in pottery easily translated to the techniques of blown glass – 'the spinning of the objects'. Monash glass is a rare scene: it is now the last remaining glass course in Victoria. Herbert was particularly taken with the technique of casting blown glass and for his production work developed chandeliers with a lighting designer.

Herbert has always been a photographer and uses his camera during travels to capture images for future inspiration. In Berlin one work of art in particular made a deep impression upon him. It was not in a gallery or museum – Herbert found it abandoned on the street. While wandering around, he came across a fridge on the side of the road. The inside of the fridge had been cast in concrete. For Herbert, it was 'like someone had experimented with something and then couldn't do anything with it'. This strange apparition formed a deep impression. It was the kind of predestined coincidence of travel that can change a life.

The seed began to grow. Herbert admired artists such as Rosalie Gasgcoine who work with found objects. But he cautions that 'You've got to be really careful what you do with [a found object], you've got to change its context ... Then I realised that I had these skills to make things into glass and that's why I should be doing it.' Soon Herbert began casting objects himself, but in glass rather than concrete.

Herbert started looking around his own neighbourhood in Yarraville, a quaint suburb in the west of Melbourne. He collected packaging materials, such as the polystyrene interiors left inside boxes that have contained consumer goods. He particularly liked damaged materials. Herbert approached this method with an almost scientific discipline. He doesn't prejudge the origins of the polystyrene shells: 'I wouldn't even know what object it contained. That's important because my judgment isn't clouded.' He meted out poetic justice across Melbourne's west.

There's something quite remarkable happening in Herbert's work. He is inverting the world, twice over. While the virtue of polystyrene is its lightness, glass has precisely the opposite quality. Herbert transforms a shape that weighs 20 grams into one weighing 40 kilograms. In addition the polystyrene form is already a negative of the object that it contained. For example, you can see from two foam shells the outline of a television that they once contained. In casting the packaging Herbert is making a negative of a negative.

To these inversions, Herbert adds the sublime dimension of colour. Combined with the dappled texture of polystyrene, Herbert grants the material form a depth of light similar to water. Like Sally Marsland, Herbert introduces colour as a creative intervention to casting. Unlike Marsland, however, Herbert is fixed to a particular form.

While his experience growing up in Malaysia had something to do with an interest in discarded objects, Herbert identifies the city of Melbourne itself as an important influence. The city has its grand boulevards such as Collins Street, but each is shadowed by a smaller street, from which lanes branch off. 'Turn the corner in the laneway and there's no one there. There might be a rusty door that hadn't been used before. Why is that abandoned?' Herbert walks through the city as though he might is combing a beach.

Herbert's cast glass forms provide contemporary consumer society with an enduring monument. Their weight offers us precious psychological ballast to help steady the effects of a constantly diverting culture.

David Herbert
Window 2003
lead crystal
13 x 30 x 10 cm
Photo: David McArthur

Anna Phillips
Cell Mass 2004
solidified shampoo, bathwater
29 x 50 x 50 cm
Photo: Jan Dallas

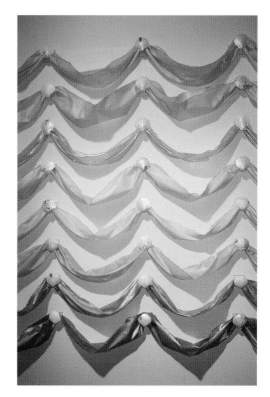

Anna Phillips
Luxe Skin 2004
Solidified shampoo, bathwater
each skin approx 30 x 20 x 1.5 mm
Photo: Jan Dallas

Chapter 4: ALCHEMISTS

Craft process can sometimes include alchemical transformation. With experience, a maker can learn how to radically change a substance, as evident in the richly varied glazes that emerge from a ceramic kiln. At the heart of this mystery is the capacity to create something precious out of ordinary materials.

While there are some materials in modern consumer items that have a definite form, many substances are less fixed in nature. As the dominant man-made substance of our times, plastic is designed to be easily transformed into different shapes and objects. The artists here are challenged to use materials not in their found manifestation, but to transform them into other objects.

Anna Phillips

The shower is one of the most ordinary experiences in a day. For a precious few minutes, bodies are lathered in sweet-smelling soaps before emerging fresh into the world of responsibilities. It takes a creative leap, though, to imagine how this fluid theatre might be transformed into a solid work of art. This is the ambition of Tasmanian artist Anna Phillips, who strives to fashion works of enduring beauty out of shampoo. How did she discover the artistic potential of shampoo? What does she make of it?

Anna Phillips working in laboratory making own shampoo combinations, Schwarzkopf, Hamburg, 2000

Phillips's alchemic quest to render fine art out of detergent involves a number of dramatic shifts. Persisting through these shifts is the artist's quirky intelligence.

It begins on the other side of the world. With a strong hint of irony, Anna describes growing up in rural Cheshire, 'on the side of a canal among the buttercups.' This English childhood was disrupted in 1969 when she joined a generation of orphaned children who were transported to Australia. 'I remember watching Neil Armstrong on the TV – thought my coming to Tasmania was a bit like the moon landing.' While it was a great shock initially, at least life here was an out from working class England. Anna's introduction to Tasmania was a children's home in the island's north, shared with her brother and sister.

Later Phillips trained as a nurse, because she 'didn't know what else to do'. It wasn't until she was thirty-three that she finally found the answer. Phillips describes spending the first half of her life 'in a daze … just doing what I was told, working in institutions and wearing starched "neck to knee" uniforms, staring out hospital windows at three in the morning'. This meaninglessness came to a head when she accidentally drove through a red light. The brush with death caused her to reconsider things.

Instinctively she drove straight on to the art school in Hunter Street, Hobart, and walked up the steps. She describes going up to the woman at the reception desk and proclaiming, 'I wish I was here.' Luckily, it was the very day they were conducting interviews for prospective students. 'Somebody must have cancelled, and they gave me their interview time, there and then … I have no regrets about that fateful day in the car. It was the best day of my life.'

At the Hobart School of Art, it was popular for students to trawl through the abandoned things found in markets and opportunity shops. It was here that the artist Julie Gough discovered her indigenous identity. She and Anna did the op-shops together, Phillips collecting Tupperware and Gough sourcing Aboriginal knick-knacks.

Phillips gathered hundreds of pastel coloured containers with opaque lids. She describes being fascinated by their 'greasy, dull, pastel shaded' plastic appearance. She was particularly attracted to plastic shampoo containers. They turned a beautiful colour when held up to the light. She was taken by the brand of Finesse shampoo, which was produced in 'electric blue plastic'. Her aim was to 'trap that magic' somehow in sculptural form.

All this time, Phillips was secretly in love with shampoo. She describes its allure: 'I love the syrupy, drippy, viscous materiality of shampoo. Its odours and colours remind me of melted silk and pearly satin materials. The way it catches the light and shimmers blobbing out into your palm, with a gentle squeeze of its malleable plastic container, then dissolves, disappears, as if just by magic.' But how to make art out of this?

A teacher advised Phillips to 'trust the materials', so she started cooking shampoo and used bathwater together – 'cooking it up in a big pan on the stove, till it was in a slow rolling boil!' She describes the process as 'very alchemical', as though she had 'stolen' the consumer magic of shampoo, and harnessed it to her own ends. 'The smells were divine! The colours were molten, reminding me of volcanic lava.' Here is a scene of elemental creation using the most artificial of substances.

After the boiling process, the shampoo halva is poured onto a host surface where it cures for up to a week. It gradually changes from being a moist, delicate skin to elastic

Anna Phillips
Nymphs 1999
shampoo bathwater and
solidifying ingredients
10 x 18 x 10 cm
Photo: Eleanor Ray

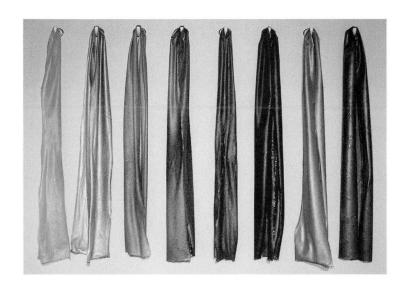 

leather. 'I felt I had managed to transform its elements and capture its magic within the solidified, set skin.'

To further refine her new craft, Phillips travelled to Hamburg on a self-initiated art research project, the aim of which was to learn to make shampoo at Schwarzkopf. She worked in a mainly German-speaking laboratory with biochemists, designers and perfumers. Rather than communicate through words, she and the staff used the language of smells. Hours were spent inhaling wonderful, mysterious fragrances; vapours wafted over them as Phillips, the frustrated perfumer, tried to find 'the right odour for a new shampoo'. Schwarzkopf kindly shipped home seventy litres of the artist's created shampoo at the completion of her residency.

The forms that Phillips creates reflect the viscous quality of her material. She draws inspiration from the American sculptor Lynda Benglis, whose work she finds 'lumpy, bumpy, almost figurative and recognisable, but at the same time grotesque and confronting'. And so, Phillips confects weird forms out of the effluent of our morning.

Her work can have a delicious irony. For an exhibition on the theme of historical Tasmanian figures, *Haven*, she created a cape for Jorgen Jorgenson, the luckless Dane who was once crowned King of Iceland, and ended up in Hobart twice, first as surveyor and second as convict. Jorgenson's megalomaniac tendencies were represented by

Above left:
Anna Phillips
Lipstick Skins 2004
solidified shampoo, bathwater, lipstick
150 x 15 x .1 cm
Photo: Jan Dallas

Above right:
Anna Phillips
Mauve Skin 2004
solidified shampoo, bathwater
variable dimensions
length approx. 300 cm
Photo: Jan Dallas

a cape made from red wine, blood, urine, Old Spice aftershave, brine and bathwater. The final garment was embossed with images of playing cards, reflecting the wearer's weakness for gambling.

With devious creativity, Phillips creates something solid out of what seems the ultimate consumable substance. The effect is more baroque than Buddhist, reflecting a seduction by materials that lurks in our consumerist unconscious.

Stephen Gallagher

We look back to the Elizabethan age as a highpoint of finery and ritual. Cartridge pleats, spiral lacing, gable hoods, coifs, partlets, embroidered motifs, ruffs, sonnets and chivalry. The English renaissance seems the antithesis of late capitalism, with its casual dress and shopping malls. But it's from such antitheses that art is born. A jeweller from Queensland has found a way of taking the most pervasive material of our consumer culture and granting it an Elizabethan elegance.

He couldn't have arisen from more unlikely beginnings. Stephen Gallagher grew up in Maryborough, a small Queensland town, just inland from Fraser Island. He

Stephen Gallagher

Facing page:
Stephen Gallagher
Double Ruff Shag Brooch 2004
Acrylic sealant, stainless steel mesh (heat treated and pressed), 925 silver (oxidised), akoya pearls, cotton thread, bakelite and red coral
15 x 15 x 2 cm
Photo: Terence Bogue

Stephen Gallagher
Perishable Jewellery Series II: group of cuffs 1997
925 silver and paper
11 x 11 x 2.6 cm
Photo: Terence Bogue

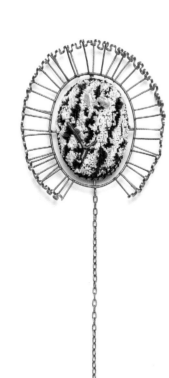

Stephen Gallagher
Pomander Pendant (front) 2004
Acrylic sealant, stainless steel mesh
(heat treated and pressed), 925 silver
(oxidised), pure gold, cotton thread,
red coral, bakelite, cultured pearls
6 x 6 x 3.4 cm (pendant only)
Photo: Terence Bogue

comes from four generations of butchers in rural Queensland but describes himself as of Australian mongrel descent, as other ancestors were German, Dutch, Spanish and Irish.

The transformative moment for Gallagher occurred while travelling through Italy. He was awe-struck by Florence – a city with 'gold and golden sunsets' – and suffering a case of Stendhal's syndrome. He was particularly impressed to see working benches on public view in the jewellery stores. A seed was sewn.

When Gallagher returned to Brisbane in 1988, he immediately started making jewellery. His lack of training and equipment was no impediment. He began making on the kitchen table, using whatever came to hand. Gallagher's first pieces were aluminium, which had the virtue of being cheap. He then started going to leadlight shops for 'bits and pieces' that he could incorporate into his work.

Jewellery for friends soon expanded into a serious occupation. He started making street jewellery for a shop in Fortitude Valley selling recycled 1950s clothing. For these pieces he used reflector tape and Perspex; they were mostly cold-joined, using screws and bolts.

Gallagher eventually enrolled in a jewellery course at Griffith University. The emphasis was on base metals, but Gallagher's primary interest was in finding ways to turn precious materials into something common, to produce alternative golds in purple, green and black.

Gallagher was influenced by the ideas and work of Japanese jeweller Kazuhiro Ito, who could make an exquisite ring out of a piece of wire. 'My belief, reflected in his work, [is] that jewellery shouldn't be taken on the monetary value of the material, as in gold, silver or platinum. That it should be in the element of design. So I try to hide the precious in material, and let the design and form of the piece speak for itself.' In a way, the more humble the material, the more salient the design.

Since the beginning, Gallagher has been looking for new techniques that will bestow elegance on modest materials. For a while he made perishable jewellery from paper and airmail stickers. A number of residencies, including a mentorship at the Victorian Embroiderers Guild, have since enabled Gallagher to include a variety of textile techniques in his jewellery. Most recently, he has been developing a series of work that strives for an Elizabethan style, though using modern materials. Gallagher is interested in the common ground between Australian motifs and Elizabethan imagery. He draws from the work of naturalists, such as the colonial Tasmanian illustrator and poet Anna Louise Meredith. With the introduction of stainless steel mesh, Gallagher is able to incorporate a kind of floral embroidery into his jewellery.

Gallagher sees an Australia that is contrary to its rough and ready stereotype. He believes that Australia was colonised in the Elizabethan spirit, evident in its history of pageantry.[19] He is attracted to the work of gothic architect Augustus Pugin in Tasmania. Gallagher's vision of Australia offers a new ground upon which to realise the aesthetic values of our imperial home while freed from the weight of traditions and hierarchy.

In work resembling Sally Marsland's flat colour brooches Gallagher extrudes acrylic caulk sealant through mesh to create dense, chaotic patterns. Rather than the forced intricacy of Elizabethan craftsmanship, Gallagher coaxes complexity from the free expression of material. The final construction of his brooches contains this chaos within a familiar form, using fittings that might be found in Elizabethan ornament.

Another series of work uses the textile technique of chenilling to create elegant brooches out of mere plastic shopping bags. By slashing black and grey plastic, Gallagher is able to create a wonderfully textured surface that belies its humble origins. For the artist, these pieces are ironic because with 'green consumerism' on the rise it is possible to conceive that plastic bags in the future will be as rare as pearls today.

Gallagher's work reflects an alchemical fascination for humble materials. The transformation of common into precious challenges the artist with a creative quest to exercise the latent mysteries of his craft.

Mark Vaarwerk

Certain crafts have had a history that seems as long as civilisation itself. Along with pottery and basketry, string making is a universal skill still practised in most traditional societies. The simple technique of spinning fibre has been used to develop a thread that can have a multitude of uses. While the skill in making string might seem archaic today, one jeweller has discovered how the technique can be used to turn contemporary trash into timeless beauty.

Mark Vaarwerk grew up in the western Sydney suburbs. Like many children of his generation, he remembers his grandparents as active artisans. His grandmother was constantly at the needle and his mother's father had a passion for carving detailed

Stephen Gallagher
Billie-O Fern 2002
Stainless steel mesh
dimensions variable
Photo: Kim Tonelli

Mark Vaarwerk
spinning strands 2004
Photo: Richard Jarvis

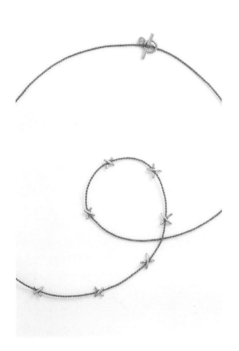

Mark Vaarwerk
Small Crosses Necklace 2004
hand-spun plastic shopping bag, 18ct gold
44 cm
Photo: Mark Vaarwerk

Facing page:
Mark Vaarwerk
Finger Rings 2004
plastic shopping bags, sterling silver,
18 carat yellow, white and pink gold
2.5 cm diameter
Photo: Mark Vaarwerk

model ships in wood. Vaarwerk's parents continued this practical interest. His father is a signwriter whose hobbies have included photography and electronics, and his mother was an expert knitter.

Of growing up, Vaarwerk remembers indulging in craft fads, such as making wooden boats and paper aeroplanes, and doing French knitting. His local area was half bush-land and half 'undeveloped suburban dumping ground'. Not a sporty type, Mark was attracted to the solitary world of plants and animals, and machines. He especially remembers 'old broken things and destructively exploring the intricate otherworld inside'. Treasures extracted included 'lenses from old cameras or projectors, and magnets from old radio speakers, lead weights from defunct piano keys, small objects extracted from ordinary things – that had their own fascinating and mysterious qual-ities.' Vaarwerk feels that this childhood experience has been of great benefit as a jeweller. It has given him the experience of using his hands and understanding how things work together.

Vaarwerk studied metalwork and woodwork at school, but did not continue these subjects. Instead, he decided to pursue a career in botany after moving to the Blue Mountains and being inspired by the diversity of plant life. After studying for a few years at the University of New South Wales, Vaarwerk was disillusioned with the amount of laboratory work involved, 'which is a far cry from the wilderness that first pointed me in the botanical direction'. We began to study silver jewellery at nights as part of an adult education course. After having found his vocation in jewellery, Vaar-werk enrolled at the Enmore Design Centre.

His first pieces were highly functional. He describes being the 'minimalist' of the class. He had a 'yearning for simplicity' and limited himself to only rudimentary and inexpensive equipment.

During this time, Vaarwerk specialised in the technique of handspinning and dye-ing with natural materials. He admits the influences of Aboriginal and Maori craft as well as the jewellery of New Zealander Warwick Freeman. A new world beckoned: 'So I learnt how to make string, using sheep, goat, rabbit, possum, alpaca, cotton, agave (cactus) and flax fibres I had collected, prepared and even grown myself, and dyeing them with plant roots or leaves, lichen, fungi, insect scale, et cetera (witches brew kinds of things).'

Mark Vaarwerk
Cubes Necklace 2004
hand-spun plastic shopping bag, second-hand
plastic bead necklaces, sterling silver
42.5 cm
Photo: Mark Vaarwerk

Mark Vaarwerk
'Polymer' Necklace 2004
hand-spun plastic shopping bag, sterling silver
43.5 cm
Photo: Mark Vaarwerk

There was no end to it. Beyond the natural world, Vaarwerk began to explore unconventional fibres, such as fur from tennis balls, tape from audio cassettes, fake fur from an old Santa Claus suit, old stuffed alligators or rabbits (the fur and the stuffing), fishing line, cloth scraps and dental floss (mint flavoured). There was something almost nanotechnological about Vaarwerk's methodology for transforming all corners of the consumable world into fibre.

Having opened up a world of possibilities, the challenge for Vaarwerk was to find his own path as an artist. He relocated to Brisbane where he was lucky to receive an Australia Council mentorship to work under the innovative jeweller Tracey Clement. By this stage, Vaarwerk had adapted spinning techniques to so he could use them with plastic bags. Without prejudice, Vaarwerk was drawn to work with plastic bags because of their bright colour, strength, durability, smoothness, flexibility and cost. As often happens in the world of 'poor crafts', friends soon assisted the artist in gathering good quality bags, often from distant places.

Vaarwerk continued to explore simple combinations of material and technique. Around this time he developed a method of beading which didn't involve drilling holes through silver beads, but rather spinning them into the plastic-like spiky seeds caught in the fleece of sheep.

Vaarwerk continues to develop the precious potential of plastic bags, and has explored the use of plastic bags in combination with precious materials, such as silver and gold. His necklaces feature silver forms bound by a string made from plastic bags. Vaarwork has also taken plastic bags beyond string into more conventional jewellery. During a residency he spent in Heckington, Lincolnshire, which was part of an exchange program between Australia and the United Kingdom, Vaarwerk turned braided plastic bags into rings by slowly melting them in an oven.

Thanks partly to a liberated childhood and adult guidance from established makers, Vaarwerk is able to use one of the most artificial elements in our environment as though it were a precious material. In this he continues the alchemic quest to transform base substance into sublime beauty. In his words, he seeks 'a discovery of familiarity and in this familiarity an unexpected beauty often unseen in everyday things – things such as plastic bags or plastic shampoo bottles'.[20]

Chapter 5: **DISSECTORS**

One way of approaching found objects is to 'save' them – to rescue them from oblivion and recover their lost meaning. But there's a negative way too. By cutting up, unravelling, carving and impressing, the artists here are able to reveal new dimensions of otherwise taken-for-granted objects. Theirs is a particularly uncertain journey, as they attempt to create by first destroying.

Louiseann Zahra

Oscar Wilde's immortal line 'We kill the thing we love' is normally understood as a statement of savage irony. There is a romantic undercurrent though. Decay and destruction can sometimes also reveal an inner beauty, in a process which is more sincere than trying to preserve something forever. A dying rose smells better than formaldehyde.

Louiseann Zahra is an artist who creates works of exquisite beauty by challenging conventions of preciousness. She has an uncanny sense of how to destroy an object, and in so doing preserve its true beauty. At the same time, she is deeply committed to art in everyday life, found wherever people bind meaning into rituals.

Louiseann was born in Traralgon, a small town in the heart of the Latrobe Valley where coal is extracted to power the state of Victoria. Her Maltese parents had practical jobs: her father was a carpenter and mother a textile designer. According to Louiseann, her parents gave her the skill to think in three-dimensional form; they encouraged her to make things with her own hands.

Bored with life in a sleepy country town, Louiseann strove initially to fill her imagination with the world of books. She read her way through the local library by the time she was fourteen and dreamt of being a writer. However, she believes her Catholic upbringing also made it easy for her to relate to the visual language of art.

After school Louiseann enrolled at Gippsland Institute of Art, where she was able to combine the study of art and literature. She then transferred to the Victorian College of the Arts and completed a Graduate Diploma in Printmaking. The formal art atmosphere at the VCA made Louiseann feel uncomfortable using the practical skills that her parents had taught her. So she created at home and made things for purely personal use.

Louiseann Zahra
studio table with Polaroid
Photo: Justin Bernhaut

Facing page:
Louiseann Zahra
*Singing the Praises of the
Man She Loves* 2002
human hair, stainless steel
and acrylic pins, glass beads
90 x 65 x 35 cm (variable)
Photo: Justin Bernhaut

Louiseann Zahra
Exposed to the Admiration of All
Before Being Consigned to the Fire 2003
bronze
Photo: Justin Bernhaut

Zahra suggests that it was travel as much as formal study that determined her course as an artist. Her first European trip coincided with a number of exhibitions by the French surrealist sculptor Louise Bourgeois. Zahra identifies Bourgeois as a 'model' for being 'a maker, in a strange, eclectic way'. For Zahra, Bourgeois was a contrast to the feminist artists of the seventies who were 'felting things' and making 'chunky work'. As a 'feisty feminist', Bourgeois enabled chance encounters between materials: 'Here's a piece of silk handkerchief and I'll pop it on a bone, and it works!' Bourgeois also made Zahra think of using metal in combination with textiles. And so in the uncanny juxtaposition of materials craft becomes art.

The Catholic basis of Zahra's work was reinforced by visiting Malta. There Zahra was struck that 'They don't worship the virgin, they worship the actual statue.' She was deeply impressed with the evidence of human bodies and other objects found in church reliquaries. 'The idea of truth, the real thing, the body's relationship to these other materials, like bones put with glass, put with gold, put with silver. These combinations were breathtakingly beautiful.' As an inherently theatrical medium, Catholicism supported a practice that sought poetic meaning in materials.

Zahra returned to Melbourne to take up a studio residency at Gertrude Contemporary Art Spaces. She now had the space and privacy to incorporate her craft skills into her art. Her first solo show at Linden gallery, *Bed*, was an exploration of scale, with over-sized objects draped in soft, knitted materials.

True to her beliefs, Zahra kept her eyes open to life beyond the art world. She spent a year working at the Melbourne University children's centre developing their creative program. Such engagement with the wider community is driven by her belief in art as a universal experience, rather than limited to a select few.

Zahra then enrolled in a masters degree at Monash University, where she pursued a number of investigations into making. On one occasion, she attempted to place an embroidered motif of a red carnation on a piece of textile. 'It was really gorgeous and exquisite – it was hideous! I couldn't believe how twee it was.' While unpicking it, she found that it was possible to remove the textile without destroying the embroidery. 'I realised that to make something else of these materials, I had to partially destroy these things as well.'

From this realisation emerged a host of new techniques, such as lost-wax casting and use of vertical weft. Fundamental to Zahra's philosophy is the concept of honouring by destroying. 'I take something that is discarded – [the things] are from op-shops and second-hand markets. I have regard of them, I understand their history. But if I was to do nothing then, they are kind of dead.' Opposite to a conservator, who strives to restore something to its original condition, Zahra seeks to radically transform the found object into something other. In this way the object is given a life that transcends its original function. It is a kind of positive deconstruction.

Zahra has cultivated a number of experiences overseas that have introduced new methods and ideas into her work. During a residency in Paris in 2001, she frequented flea markets. She was amazed to see the range of goods on display and the obvious depth of history. She saw whole seventeenth-century trousseaus laid out on the street.

The flea market became her palette. Zahra started collecting obscure objects of lost beauty, such as chandelier fragments. But her attention strayed from made objects. While wandering outside Sacre Coeur, she encountered a number of Africans selling human hair. She subsequently tried to crochet hair, but to work it found that she had to lick the material. 'All my friends were worried I was going to develop mouth ulcers. But nothing happened.' She was particularly intrigued by ancient hair, such as that on the bodies in the Parisian catacombs. The material 'life' of mortality fascinated Zahra.

In 2003 she visited Mexico and experienced *Los Días de los Muertos*, the Day of the Dead. She was attracted to this festival partly out of her belief that 'all objects should be considered art'. The event involved the construction of ephemeral objects such as candies and tin votives; these are destroyed in the course of the rituals. Zahra described the objects made for the ceremonies as 'almost rubbish', but noted they had deep symbolic content.

The exhibition *The Dead Are Never Lonely* (Craft Victoria, 2003) emerged out of Zahra's Mexican experience. Her installations incorporated found popular objects that celebrate death, such as plastic skeletons and tin melagra (representations of body parts). The black walls of the exhibition space were strewn with monumental garlands of marigold. In amongst them was a necklace made from used wedding rings. Lying on the floor were feathers cast in bronze, titled 'exposed to the admiration of all before being consigned to the fire'. Zahra evoked a sense of human destiny through material transformation.

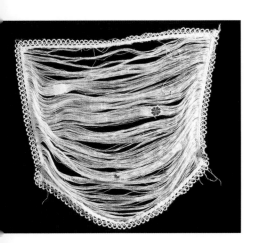

Louiseann Zahra
If He So Intended 2002
cotton, velvet (framed)
62 x 80 x 4 cm
Photo: Justin Bernhaut

Louiseann Zahra
Noting My Interest Was Feigned 2001
cotton, blood
90 x 110 x 3 cm
Photo: Justin Bernhaut

Casting is a technique that suits Zahra particularly well. It enables her to reflect on the ephemeral nature of beauty in everyday life. On one occasion, her mother made sugar flowers for a wedding cake. Zahra found them so exquisite that she decided to cast them. Now that she is living in Footscray, Zahra collects many of the plastic ornaments sold in the markets. She describes the suburb as 'plastic fantastic'. After casting plastic flowers Zahra places them under glass domes that make the objects seem like precious museum pieces.

Continuing to push the edges of art, Zahra is particularly intrigued by the potential of blood as an artistic material. One of her many experiments was an attempt to paint with blood. Unable to find someone who would agree to draw her own blood, she was forced to use fresh duck's blood from a local Vietnamese restaurant. She found blood hard to work with because the clear yellowish plasma separated out . Certain other aspects of working with the substance disturbed her, such as accidentally

Facing page:
Nicholas Jones
Bookscape VII 2004
carved book
23 x 14.5 x 2.5 cm
Photo: Paul Batt

Nicholas Jones
Book In Flight ('The Hero of St Roger')
2004
folded book
27.3 x 25 x 11 cm
Photo: Paul Batt

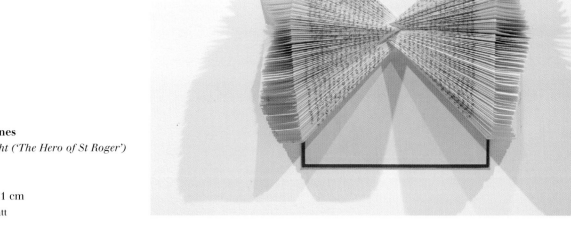

Nicholas Jones

splashing blood on herself while working, and having to re-wet the fabrics she was painting, in order to stop the blood turning 'crunchy'.

For Zahra, the preciousness of life is most evident in its passing. It is the remainders of life, particularly the materiality that is cast off from the mortal frame, that provide her with her creative stock. As death levels all, so Zahra finds beauty in the everyday world around her.

Nicholas Jones

As Hegel would say, 'The owl of Minerva flies at dusk.' So the guiding concept of an era often becomes apparent as it is coming to a close. Many have thought along these lines in contemplating the meaning of the book. The biblical foundation of Judeo-Christian civilisation was expressed in the phrase 'people of the book' applied to both Jews and Christians. In the twenty-first century the book is no longer the primary means by which information is stored. The book is evolving from a repository of knowledge to a thing in itself. Information migrates from printed pages to electronic databases. We move from the Bible to the Human Genome Project.

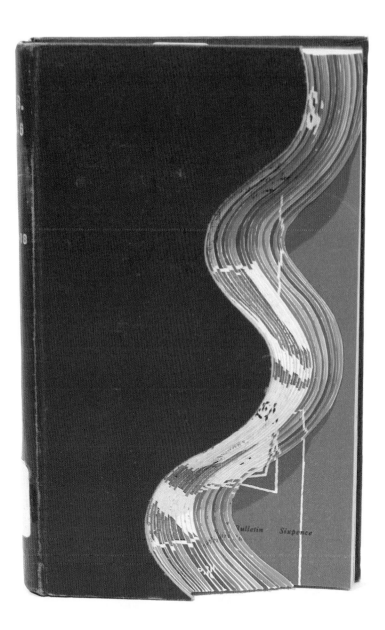

What then becomes of books? It is perhaps now that we can truly appreciate them as objects in their own right. So Paul Duguid, writing on the 'Past and futurology of the book', describes the book as if it were a machine: 'The closed cover, the turned page, broken spine, serial form, immutable text, revealing heft, distinctive formats, handy size ... '[21] As we become less reliant on books for the storage of information, we release them for other uses, particularly aesthetic.

It is timely, then, for an artist such as Nicholas Jones to develop a specific set of techniques for realising the inner beauty of books – even if this beautification involves their destruction.

Jones came across the idea of carving books while studying at the Victorian College of the Arts. His teacher of the time, Elizabeth Presa, was working with paper in unusual ways, combining it with wax and making clothes. Jones initially began with techniques of sewing and tearing. By 1999 he had begun folding the pages of books as well.

Jones is often attentive not just to the re-fashioned book, but also where it sits. He follows the model of Brancusi, who strove to make the plinth as beautiful as the finished object placed upon it. Jones often utilises the cover of the hardback book to provide a backdrop to the re-worked contents.

There are a number of effects that Jones aims for. He uses the ageing property of paper to create gradations of colour, from white to yellow. By cutting into the pages of a book, he is able to expose the text and create a stippled texture. Jones sees his work as a kind of concrete poetry.

Jones sources his books mostly at opportunity shops. Growing up around the Camberwell Market, in Melbourne's east, gave him an appreciation of second-hand goods. At the same time, he is often called upon to provide a repository for those contemplating a book clearance. University High School once delivered to him a truckload of books about to be pulped.

Jones settled on the idea of becoming an artist while studying fine arts at La Trobe University. During a tutorial on Attic vases, Jones thought 'Either I can become someone who works in the field of art history, or I can work hard and get into TAFE and uni and make my own work that people will be talking about.' So he launched from theory to practice.

While art school shaped his ambition, his specific expression stems from an experi-

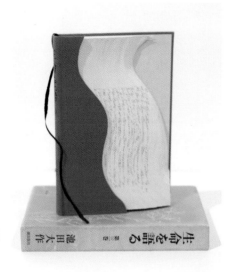

Nicholas Jones
High Coup 2002
carved book set on its dust box
22.5 x 20 x 14 cm
Photo: Paul Batt

Nicholas Jones
Wormwood 2003
torn and sewn found paper
with linen thread
17 x 32 x 26 cm
Photo: Paul Batt

ence that he had when much younger. At the age of five, Jones watched his surgeon father perform an appendicectomy on a thirteen-year-old boy. Since then, Jones has been fascinated by medical instruments. He now calls himself a 'book surgeon' and attempts to apply the same care to dissecting books as his father did to operating on patients.

The scalpel has now become the artist's most used instrument. Jones has considered using power tools, such as a drill, to make the process of his work easier. But like human flesh, paper is too delicate for anything other than a sharp, hand-held blade.

Jones's work makes quite a spectacle. During a residency in 2003 Jones spent a month working inside a gallery and performing his craft. Making his work accessible to the public in this way generated interesting responses. Jones sat at a bench surrounded by a sea of potential victims – condemned books lying on the floor. Many visitors pleaded with him to spare a particular volume that had evoked their pity. They would seek reprieve for a particular book by offering their own books as substitutes.

Jones is shaping to be a kind of artistic conscience for the electronic age. Like Rose-anne Bartley who used typewriter keys in her brooches, Jones finds the beauty in the remnants of the print age.

Tiffany Parbs

Well used, the deconstructive method has the capacity to take us to places that are both disarmingly familiar and happily strange. Tiffany Parbs has settled on one of the dark secrets of jewellery – so obvious that we never even considered it a secret.

Most jewellery worn on the body is not entirely innocent. Metal objects leave a trace, though it might only be temporary. A ring will leave a red circle around the finger; a clip-on earring compresses the lobe, and a brooch loosens the fibre of our clothing. Rather than jewellery itself, Parbs works on the traces it leaves – 'the way the marks resonate on the skin long after the pieces have been removed'. Hers is a daring journey.

Parbs has explored different techniques for turning skin into jewellery. One technique was to make rashes on the skin using a series of pins. Her focus is less about the object, and more about the mark it creates on the skin. Recent work is inspired by associations with particular words: "itch", "bruise", "burn", "scar", "pucker" and "clamp". Like others in this generation of makers, Parbs opens a door into a realm of unacknowledged adornment.

Tiffany Parbs in her studio
Photo: Samuel MacGeorge

Tiffany Parbs
Pincers 2002
stainless steel, sterling silver,
German silver, brass
variable dimensions
Photo: Michael Kluvanek

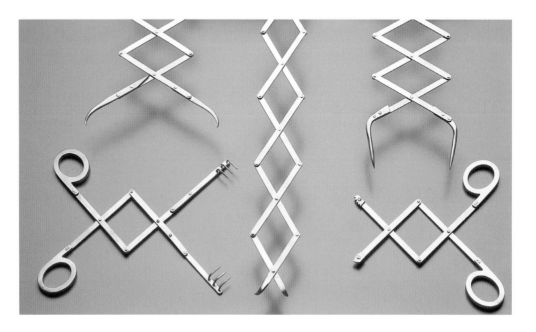

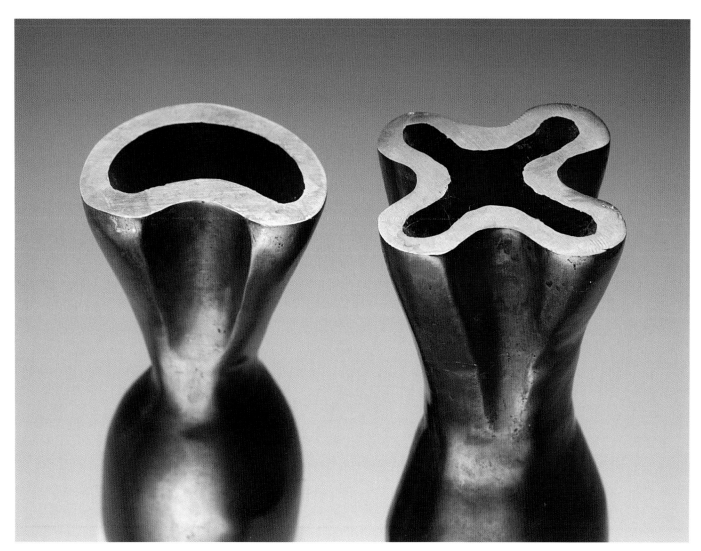

Tiffany Parbs
Skin Stamps (detail) 2002
brass, patina
3.4 x 2.5 x 8.5 cm
Photo: Michael Kluvanek

Tiffany Parbs
Rash Stamps 2004
sterling silver, nickel-plated pins
5.3 x 3.5 x 1.3 cm
Photo: Greg Harris

As with many idiosyncratic artists, the inspiration for her art stems from a childhood experience. Tiffany grew up in the Barossa Valley. Her family ran a saw mill, started by her grandfather. Her father is a saw doctor, and she grew up surrounded by big, heavy machinery – 'I've been surrounded by precision'. There is a strong interest in tools to this day.

As a child, Tiffany had close contact with a number of relatives who had suffered radical surgery. Her grandfather had lost both legs. During her daily visits, he would make the surreal request of his grandchild that she scratch his invisible foot. This uncanny ritual was reinforced by other experiences, such as witnessing the effects of a mastectomy and nasalectomy. These are the kinds of memories that lie in wait for some kind of expression in later life.

After finishing school, Parbs began by enrolling in a course of Communication Studies, which she found too theoretical. While in Sydney, she met someone studying jewellery at the North Adelaide School of Art. Parbs subsequently went to an information session, heard the ceramicist Gerry Wedd and was 'hooked'. She had found her path. Parbs did a three-year advanced diploma at the South Australian art school. She was particularly supported by the jeweller Don Ellis, who encouraged her to approach the Gray Street Workshop when she left the course.

Parb's graduating work was quite theatrical. She employed cast brass to make

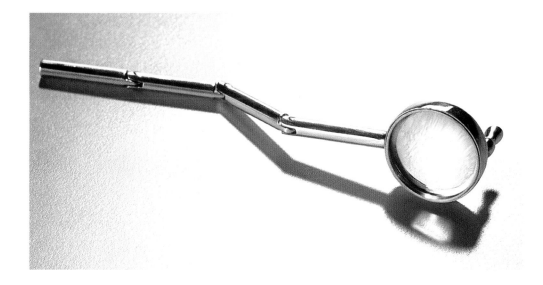

Tiffany Parbs
Skin Magnifier 2002
sterling silver, lens, German silver
13.2 x 2.7 x 1.6 cm
Photo: Michael Kluvanek

works, such as one titled *Love Bites*, based on the theme of sexual innuendo. The artist's childhood experiences were beginning to surface and she gathered materials 'at hand'. She made a piece from her grandfather's porcelain dentures. Her father had his gold fillings replaced and gave the originals to her. The family medical history contributed directly to her work.

The Gray Street Workshop in Adelaide is one of the hubs of craft in Australia. The core group of Julie Blyfield, Leslie Matthews, Sue Lorraine and Catherine Truman have established a studio where the role of jewellery as a language of self is explored. There is particular emphasis on the relationship between jewellery and human anatomy. Sue Lorraine's steel organs and Catherine Truman's carved limewood muscles render the interior body in beautiful form. While Parbs's work has a similar focus on the body, she engages with it rather more directly than these other artists.

During her time at Gray Street, Parbs further developed her theatrical style through opportunities outside galleries. She made chastity belts for the Gay and Lesbian Mardi Gras, a series of work with the title *Cold Hearted Bitch* and another series titled *Home Enema Kit*. Her work for exhibition was still to develop.

Parbs travelled to the United Kingdom in 1997, and took up a residency at the Jewellery and Silversmithing Department of the Glasgow School of Art. She started her research into surgical instruments at the Playford Museum of Anatomy and Patho-

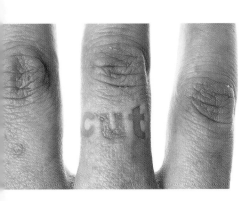

Tiffany Parbs
Etched (Cut) 2004
skin
Photo: Greg Harris

logy in the Edinburgh Surgeon's Hall. She was fascinated by the bodily condition of apotemnophilia, in which a person has a desire to amputate their limbs. Inspired by the collection Parbs started to develop self-surgery kits based on instruments from the eighteenth and nineteenth centuries. However, she was more interested in suggested use, than real use.

From this emerged the exhibition *Probe*, which used the wearer's skin as a canvas. The show included *Skin Stamps* that could be pressed onto flesh to leave differently shaped marks. There were rings that magnified the surface of the skin, revealing hairs and pores. *Alternate Skin* contained other skins that could be worn over one's own.

The very idea of jewellery implies something lacking in the body. The jewel's sparkling durability contrasts with the corruptible flesh it adorns. Parbs deconstructs this opposition by using skin itself as the jewel.

It is a jewellery of the make-over age. However, rather than celebrate the newly forged perfect being, Parbs undermines our body image with what we might call 'the real' – the part of physical being that doesn't fit neatly into either our inside or outside. Thus the Melbourne academic Justin Clements celebrates in Parbs's work what Friedrich Nietzsche called 'festive cruelty'.[22] Parbs's objects have the capacity to 'unnerve'.

After *Probe*, Parbs spent fifteen months at the Jam Factory Metal Studio, where Sue Lorraine was Head of Studio. Parbs particularly enjoyed working with sterling silver, but felt that its coldness required something warm. Skin seemed the natural material. Rather than consider the silver in isolation from the body, she was interested to find ways in which they might interact.

Parbs is a highly individual artist who has emerged in the broader context of conceptual jewellery. She admits to a wide range of influences. For instance, she has been inspired by the conceptual jewellers of the 1970s, such as Geis Bekker and Otto Kunzli, who were not afraid to create ephemeral work. A mentorship with Melbourne jeweller Susan Cohn helped develop Parbs's critical eye for technical and conceptual matters.

Parbs continues on a course to find ways of using the changeable appearance of skin as a form of ornament. In doing so she reminds us that we are the very ground on which the precious thing called jewellery rests. Jewellery is part of a dialectic between the timeless metal and our fickle flesh. Parbs's deconstructive turn renews this relationship.

Chapter 6: **LIBERATORS**

This final chapter examines a group of artists who address the relationship between common and precious in a more radical way. Rather than work with the commonness of materials themselves, these makers explore how space is organised in order to distinguish between what is valuable and what is not. Their focus is on public space, which in most Western countries is associated with commonness. Public transport, public hospitals, and the street, represent ordinariness and are distinguished from private services. The artists here invert the relationship between the public and the common by taking preciousness into the public domain.

Caz Guiney

Compared with visual art, craft more often finds itself in the thick of everyday life. Rather than hang on a wall, removed beyond the reach of daily business, a cup or chair plays a tangible role in everyday life. In the case of jewellery the wearer's body is the platform on which the work is displayed. So through jewellery artists can take their work directly onto the streets. Few have realised the potential of this as much as jeweller-*provocatrice* Caz Guiney.

Guiney has taken a critical eye to the whole precious business of jewellery. She has made rings out of the most common materials imaginable, and has caused a near-riot by casting jewels to the crowd. Her career is one of gentle, but maddeningly persistent, questioning.

Like many makers Guiney began doing something else. She started by studying Orthoptics, the measurement of vision, at Melbourne's Lincoln Institute. She then moved to Interior Design for something more creative, but she still missed the hands-on contact with materials. Guiney says: '[Making is] one of the few times that my mind doesn't drift and I'm not having three conversations in my head at once ... I'm right there with the dirt or the plastic, or the metal, or the fabric, or whatever it is.' Like other practitioners of 'poor craft' Guiney is possessed by the spirit of making.

Guiney finally studied Jewellery and Metalsmithing at the Frankston campus of Monash University, under the tutelage of Beatrice Schlabowsky and Mark Edgoose. Both these silversmiths were modernist-inspired and had rigorous methods. Guiney considers herself lucky to have had this training: 'Once you have competence with

Caz Guiney

Caz Guiney
Kinetic brooch on bin 2003
18ct yellow gold
4 x 4 cm
Photo: Andrew Barcham

Caz Guiney
Acrylic Bracelet 2000
acrylic, stainless steel springs
8 x 3 cm
Photo: Terence Bogue

Facing page:
Caz Guiney
*Telescopering on building
overlooking Flinders St Station* 2003
925 silver
2 x 3 cm
Photo: Andrew Barcham

those [techniques], you could experiment with whatever you like.' Yet her path would stray from traditional craft.

Guiney found herself more interested in the conceptual side of jewellery making. Melbourne has a strong conceptual scene, led by artists such as Susan Cohn and Robert Baines, whose work questions the role of gold in jewellery. Guiney was similarly awkward with the dependence on precious materials. When she first started production work, she found that the more gold or silver a piece of jewellery contained, the easier it was to sell.

Guiney could not brook this idolatry: 'It was a reaction to that, which pushed me to experiment with other materials and try to elevate them to the same level as gold and silver.' As expensive materials, gold and silver did not lend themselves to risk-taking. Guiney was also concerned about the environmental impact of mining: 'The statistics of the amount of earth that they have to mine to get a gram of gold is quite phenomenal. If you put yourself in that head space as a jeweller, it's really challenging.' Alternatives had to be found.

The first material she experimented with was soap. For Guiney, use of an ephemeral medium challenged the very idea of jewellery, and particularly its role as an heirloom that promises longevity. For her 1998 exhibition *Ordinary ... Orthodox ... Absurd* Guiney extended her range of materials to almost ridiculous lengths.

The 'ordinary' included rings made from foam, wood, wire mesh, soap and glass. 'Orthodox' materials were gold and silver. And 'absurd' materials included dirt, sand, grass, pumice, medication, Viagra, ground chilli, black pepper, polenta and sesame seeds. For the artist, it was an opportunity to discover beauty in the most humble of materials: 'You get to look at the pieces of dried chilli and see how beautiful they are.' The most extreme piece was a ring made of ice that soon became a pool of water – 'People [were] coming across a pool of water and wondering what on earth it was.' In Guiney's exhibition the ring as a formal device played a function similar to that of the Japanese haiku – it was a precise framework for focusing on the fleeting moment.

One practical issue with conceptualism is the problem of selling work. Despite the obvious market for gold and silver, Guiney attempted to maintain her scepticism towards preciousness in her production work. She began working with dyed plastic. She made angular bracelets with layers of tapered coloured plastic that subtly reflected the light.

Guiney's next step was the boldest. Rather than denying preciousness, she decided that the best means of combating idolatry is to embrace it. She went right to the root of the matter: her target was not gold or silver, but the individual ego. As an ornament, jewellery is designed to flatter its host. While that host is usually a person, jewellery can also cast an aura in a gallery space or even architecturally on a building. Like Frodo in *Lord of the Rings*, Guiney decided to cast this preciousness into the void.

For Guiney, the outside world was just as deserving of ornament as the human body – 'whether it's a pile of pigeon shit that makes an amazing texture, or a pile of rubbish in the corner, or a cracked window that's just covered in years and years of grime'. Thus she devised *City Rings* in 2003. Guiney located various sites in the city of Melbourne that afforded opportunities for adornment, but kept a scale that was relevant to the human body. Jewellery included silver and gold bolts attached to scaffolding, a ring set into the base of a wooden platform in the city square (a 'tree ring'), a diamond ring at the end of an air-conditioning pipe, and a kinetic ring with moving parts set into a street trash bin. It was the latter work which created most public interest.

The media took up the story as one of a waste of taxpayer resources – after all, Caz Guiney was throwing gold into the bin! *City Rings* became the subject of tabloid dailies

Caz Guiney
Ice Ring H$_2$O 1998
H$_2$O
2.2 x 1.5 cm
Photo: Andrew Barcham

Caz Guiney
Ring Sand 1998
builders' sand
2.2 x 1.5 cm
Photo: Andrew Barcham

and radio talkback. Guiney describes the worst moment as the morning when repor-
ters from the investigative television program *A Current Affair* came knocking on her
door at 8 a.m. Looking back, Guiney considers that she might have been a little naïve.

Another unanticipated effect was the treasure hunt that ensued. In an almost atavis-
tic manner *City Rings* re-awakened gold fever in Melbourne, the city founded upon
the spoils of the 1850s gold rush. Young men climbed buildings to claim a precious piece
of jewellery as a trophy. For a while, it seemed that Guiney might be responsible for
any damage they caused, or injury they might sustain. But gold fever died down as
most of the jewellery was soon souvenired.

Where does this persistent iconoclasm emerge from? While Guiney does not
come from an artistic background, her childhood contained that freedom of space
which seems critical in opening up imagination. Guiney's grandfather taught tennis
in a court on the top of a building in Melbourne's Flinders Lane. His sons followed in
the footsteps of his tennis shoes, and one settled in the suburb of Balwyn, where he was
able to construct a large tennis court by combining several blocks of land. Growing
up on this property, Caz remembers having the run of an old creek bed, and playing
in a nearby clay pit where she made pinch pots.

Flowing through her family life is an Irish sensibility that is sceptical of formality.
Her father is a jazz musician: 'Whatever he can touch he can play, clarinet, piano,
guitar – just got the mind that understands the engineering of music.' There's some-

Caz Guiney
*Two men sitting with ring on wooden
board* 2003
925 Silver, 18ct yellow gold
2.5 x 2 cm
Photo: Andrew Barcham

thing jazz-like in the way Guiney embraces the street in her work.

With the birth of her child, Guiney quietened momentarily, and began to experiment with sticky tape and wood shavings. She remains focused on working with non-precious materials: 'Each time you do it, there's something new there.' Guiney's work demonstrates how questioning the hierarchy of precious materials can make an impact on public consciousness.

Honor Freeman

Graffiti has lately been reclaimed as a form of public expression. The 'tagging' popular in the late twentieth century was designed specifically to communicate inside knowledge. To an outsider, tags were ugly scribbles defacing public property. After the turn of the millennium, however, a new art form emerged – that of stencilling. Beautifully crafted and witty stencilled images began appearing on brick walls in alleys. Such graffiti is a fresh and engaging way to bring art into everyday life.

We are beginning to now see the broad influence of this trend in more conventional arts. Stencils are appearing as forms of decoration on ceramics, for instance. This is a welcome, fresh influence in craft but it tames the public spirit of the graffiti art form. More reflective of the revolutionary spirit is the work of an Adelaide artist who has found ways of sneaking the aesthetic into our profane world through a new kind of public ceramics – faux porcelain.

Honor Freeman began with the quest to make an entirely faux porcelain world – a room where every feature would be porcelain. While this dream remains to be realised, a host of individual works have emerged. Freeman's *Milky White Melt* series included *Comfort Cups*, which are thrown forms glazed in a soft satin white with gentle dents for ease of hold. Her *Disposable* series included *White with One*, a reproduction of the most humble of objects – the used polystyrene coffee cup – in precious porcelain. Freeman also produced porcelain sponges – common, disposable kitchen items rendered in lasting form.

As well as everyday objects, Freeman makes work that reflects on common activities such as cleaning. She produced a series of *Boot Polish Beakers* which she decorated using the method her father taught her to clean shoes. While the results resembled abstract landscape painting, she was more interested in the process of mark-making as an expression of our common interaction with objects. A job cleaning a 'dodgy

Honor Freeman in her studio
Photo: Lauren Simeoni

Facing page:
Honor Freeman
On/Off/On (detail) 2002
porcelain powerpoint on
gather outside Jam Factory
Adelaide
Photo: Honor Freeman

budget motel' inspired her to think how drudgery can become meditative.

Freeman loves the immediacy of slip-casting. She is particularly intrigued by the mimetic qualities of porcelain. For her, it's a way of reaching into the taken-for-granted domain: 'So many people appear to measure their life by the big events, whereas it's the smaller moments that are a continuous rhythm throughout our everyday.'

The most radical feature of her faux porcelain world lay in the fine detail. During her mania for casting, Freeman reproduced ordinary devices such as power points and light switches. She was particularly attracted to these 'simple, humble and mundane objects'. And she was interested in 'activities that we take for granted and which go by unnoticed'. She particularly liked dealing with something that is so much part of the grain of everyday life as flicking a switch. Suggesting the solid feel of porcelain instead of the thin feel of plastic offered 'a subtle shift in the day'.

Unlike conventional artists, who strive to have their work noticed by as many people as possible, Freeman seeks inconspicuousness. Her disposition and methods do not suit industrial design. Plastic and porcelain are virtually identical to look at; the difference is in the touch. So how does Freeman make work that can mean something to the viewer? Fortunately, in mid-2002 Freeman was living with a group who did graffiti using stickers and stencils. She was inspired to go out and quietly put her *On/Off/On* porcelain switches on the street.

Freeman placed her public works around the Adelaide central business district: in telephone booths, on vending machines, at bus stops, in alley ways, at pedestrian crossings and on the sides of buildings. They were sometimes in unexpected places, and other times just where you'd expect – though not in porcelain. Most passers-by did not register their presence, at least not until their gaze wandered. Freeman says, 'I saw them as small, quiet gifts to those who notice the smaller and more subtle details in life.' It was art for those who were looking for art.

Freeman's public craft is a remarkable gift. Its significance is a product of its very insignificance. Normally, the interior world is exposed through obvious frames, such as doors and windows. One of the subliminal markers of an interior space is access to electric power. Because of the issues of billing, there is no outlet for electricity on the street. Freeman's switches turn this sharply demarcated world inside out.

As Caz Guiney did in her *City Rings* project, Freeman uses her craft to change the way

Facing page:
Honor Freeman
On/Off/On (detail) 2003
installations around streets
porcelain
Photo: Honor Freeman

people look at public space. She overturns the opposition between precious private and common public. In an age when collective forms of empowerment are rare her work is a gentle reminder of the revolutionary possibility that lies dormant.

Freeman remains true to her upbringing. Honor grew up in Bordertown, where South Australia meets Victoria. Her father was a truck driver who worked for the local abattoirs and her mother was a nurse. Honor remembers her mother always having a tape measure around her neck and a mouth full of pins; she introduced Honor to 'a craft way of making and thinking'.

Honor grew up as an only child. She had much time on her own, which she filled with daydreams, intrigued by ordinary objects around her. 'I remember writing lots of stories about toothbrushes and their adventures down the drain.'

Bordertown did not have much to offer anyone who was not interested in a job at either the road-house or meatworks. Honor remembers her art room at high school as 'an old Nissen hut that was overflowing with weird and wonderful things'. It was in her second year at the South Australian School of Art in Adelaide that Freeman discovered glass and ceramics. The sense of community in the department particularly appealed to her. But it was only in third year that she realised clay suited the way she wanted to make work: it was solitary, quiet and calm.

Freeman continues to support her artistic practice with a job cleaning in a budget motel. This most ordinary of scenes is the inspiration for recent work. Her series of work titled *Shape of a Day* memorialises the stains that are left in a motel room like intimate messages for future guests. As Freeman writes, 'The turnover in a motel sometimes makes it feel like you're sleeping with a stranger or strangers … the bed is still warm while the next guest checks in … '. Though not designed for public viewing, this latest series of work continues Freeman's interest in the uncertain boundaries between public and private. In the public domain Freeman has begun placing porcelain versions of the tags used to date packaged bread around the city of Adelaide.

Since Freeman discovered clay, the most common of creative materials, her work has evolved to bring the mystery of ceramics into commodified urban lives. Instead of the slippery nothing of plastic she offers us the hard resonance of high-fired porcelain. It's an almost subliminal effect with the potential to powerfully alter our disposition to the world.

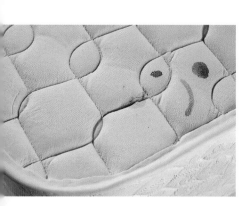

Honor Freeman
Shape Of A Day (detail) 2004
porcelain, cotton thread
Photo: Michael Kluvanek

CONCLUSION

This generation of artists is unique. Their sensibilities can be traced back to the make-do traditions of folk crafts, forged as a response to boredom and necessity. The artists featured in this book have been able to sustain this rural sensibility within an urban entertainment culture – through their personal passion for making and their discovery of a new conceptual base for contemporary craft.

This inventiveness is a rare disposition. In an age when necessity is about the only element not in abundance the artists' commitment to making do with what's available is a self-motivated creative dispensation.

In making the common precious these artists are reversing the relationship between gallery and supermarket. They give meaning to substances that would otherwise be taken for granted as the stuff of consumption – whether it is the grass beneath our

Honor Freeman
White With One 2002
porcelain
24 x 10 x 11 cm
Photo: Michael Kluvanek

feet, an outmoded typewriter, the packaging we throw away, shampoo destined for the drain, old books or the public domain itself. They bring art into life and thus make possible a form of reflection on the manic business of consumption.

To return to our original metaphor, these makers represent the last fruit of a native tree that grows only in the wild. With proliferating technologies such as Gameboys and iPods designed to fill every spare minute it seems unlikely that childhoods today have the kind of space necessary for developing a craft spirit.

But craft will continue to be relevant, while we still have bodies. Multimedia really only engages two senses: hearing and seeing. There will always be room for arts that engage the mysterious realm of touch. The tactile sense has the capacity to break through the prefabricated work of image and sound. The practitioners of 'poor craft' speak to our bodies and bypass the saturated information senses.

In straying from traditional materials the artists here challenge established schools of craft practice. For many of them, the field of textiles provides a particularly rich repertoire of techniques, particularly as applied to other media, such as ceramics, plastic and jewellery. Seeking to give craft a new relevance to contemporary life, the artists here have also diversified the craft skills to the extent of creating new schools of applied arts. This trend is likely to continue as artists find new applications for traditional techniques.

As an especially Australian phenomenon, 'poor craft' has an interesting future. It has arisen in a country situated in the part of the world where necessity is in abundance – there is poverty in the remote villages of Indonesia, the *favela*s of Rio and the vibrant townships of Johannesburg. Often, the folk crafts in these places are standardised into mass production, such as bowls woven from telephone wire vessels seen throughout South Africa. Australian artists have the opportunity to engage with surrounding communities – to exercise their virtues of necessity and also reach out beyond the white fortress.

'Poor craft' has a potentially rich future, yet it depends on the imagination of viewers to see value in what may previously have been thought worthless. It is to be hoped that the various stories collected here will help bring readers into the world of the makers, to glimpse the radical mystery at work and the adventure at the heart of the crafts practice.

Facing page:
Kate Campbell-Pope
Bronchial tree/Larynx 2002
pith cane, silk, stitched grasses
100 x 50 x 11 cm
Photo: f22 Photography

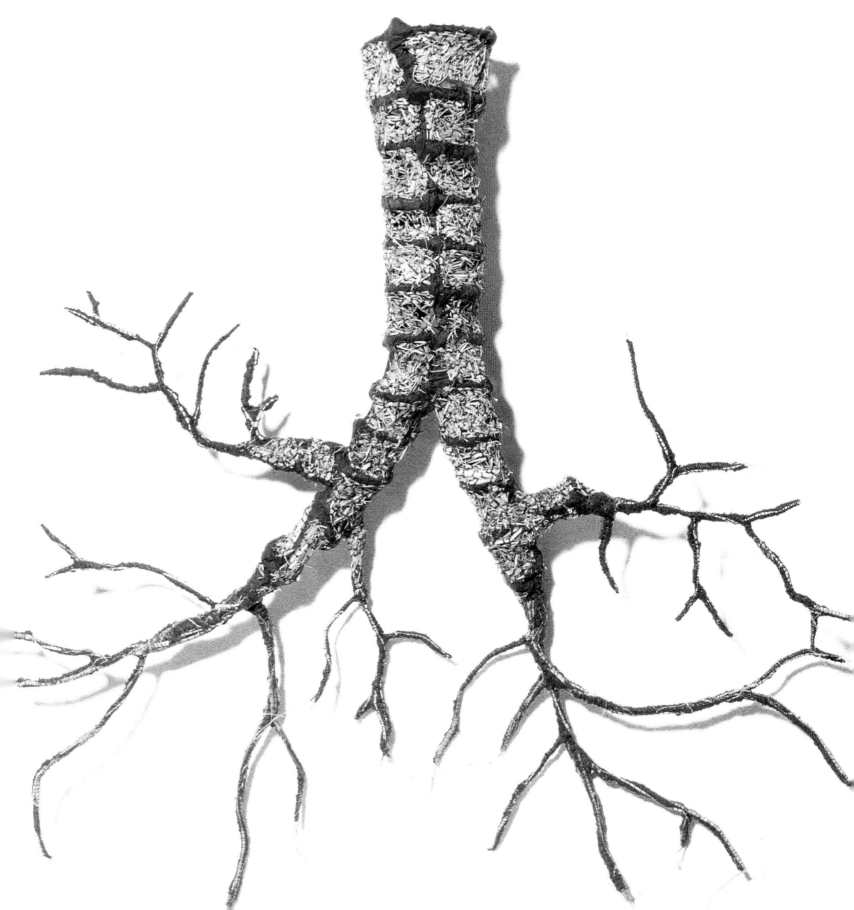

Footnotes:

1   Pierre Bourdieu, *Distinction: A Social Critique of the Judgement of Taste*, trans. R. Nice, Harvard University Press, Cambridge, Mass., 1984 (orig. 1974)

2   While the celebration of the common occurs in many different cultures and histories, we need not assume that it is linked to a universal meaning. The championing of ordinary seems a reaction against authority that emerges within a specific context.

3   John Ruskin, *Arata Pentelici: Seven Lectures on the Elements of Sculpture*, George Allen, London, 1890, p. 23.

4   Soetsu Yanagi, *The Unknown Craftsman: A Japanese Insight into Beauty*, trans. Bernard Leach, Kodansha International, Tokyo, 1989 (orig. 1931), p. 101.

5   Pierre Lévy, *Collective Intelligence: Mankind's Emerging World in Cyberspace*, Plenum Press, New York, 1997 (orig. 1995), p. 100.

6   Germano Celant, *Arte Povera: Art from Italy, 1967–2002*, Museum of Contemporary Art, Sydney, 2002, p. 23.

7   Robin Boyd, *The Australian Ugliness*, Cheshire, Melbourne, 1960, p. 16.

8   *Mambo: Still Life with Franchise*, Mambo Graphics, Sydney, 1998, p. 115

9   Alan Feinstein, *Pablo Neruda: A Passion for Life*, Bloomsbury, New York, 2004, p. 379.

10   Njabulo Ndebele, *South African Literature and Culture: Rediscovery of the Ordinary*, Manchester University Press, Manchester, 1994, p. 57. The phrase was echoed in the opening of a speech made by Mbulelo Mzamane in 2004 at a gathering of artists and writers from the southern hemisphere (see <www.southproject.org>).

11   At Jan Murphy Gallery, Brisbane, and at e.g.etal, Melbourne, 2002.

12   Chris McConville, Michael Small & Damien Wright, *A History of the Footscray Football Club*, Aus-Sport Enterprises P/L, 1996.

13   Biographical statement for Contents Forum, Craft ACT, Canberra, 2004.

14   Kate Grenville, *The Idea of Perfection*, Picador, Sydney, 1999, p. 9.

15   Statement for exhibition at Geelong Wool Museum, 2002.

16   Anna Sanderson in essay for *Almost Black*, Funaki Gallery, 2002.

17   Alex Selenitsch, review of Marsland's *Why Are You Like This and Not Like That?* in *Craft Culture*, Craft Victoria, 2004 (see www.craftculture.org/review/selenitsch4.htm).

18   Liner notes for Brian Eno, *Discrete Music*, Editions eg, 1975.

19   Janet Gleeson, *Arcanum: The Extraordinary True Story of the Invention of European Porcelain*, Bantam, London, 1998, p. x.

20   As Robert Dixon has noted (in *The Course of Empire: Neo-classical Culture in New South Wales, 1788–1860*, Oxford University Press, Melbourne, 1986) while Australia was obviously colonised after the Elizabethan era, its early settlement could be seen as informed by a neoclassical sentiment. So, says Dixon (p.3), the *Australian Magazine* in 1838 could include the verse 'And life a goddess, glittering from the deep,/Hereafter sway the sceptre of domain/From pole to pole, and such as now thou art,/Perhaps New Holland be.'

21   Artist's statement, 2004.

22   Paul Duguid, 'Material matters: The past and futurology of the book', in *The Future of the Book*, ed. G. Nunberg, University of California Press, Berkeley, 1996, p. 64.

23   'Tiffany Parbs's Probing Jewellery' (see <www.craftculture.org/archive/probe.htm>).

Facing page:
Stephen Gallagher
Group of Three Pinking Brooches 2004
plastic (chenilled), cotton thread,
stainless steel, 925 silver (oxidised)
large: 20.5 x 18 x 5 cm
medium: 15.5 x 15.5 x 2.5 cm
small: 11 x 11 x 2.5 cm
Photo: Terence Bogue

Roseanne Bartley
Heaven on a stick (Brooch) and
Seventh Heaven (Neck piece) 2004
paddle popstick, 925 silver, stainless steel
9.5 x 9.5 cm, 1.5 x 63 cm
Photo: Terence Bogue

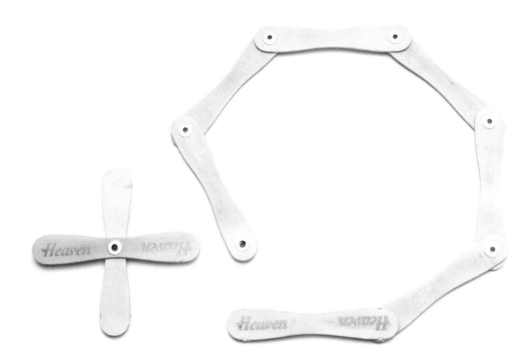